Posthuman Suffering and the Technological Embrace

Posthuman Suffering and the Technological Embrace

ANTHONY MICCOLI

LEXINGTON BOOKS
A division of
ROWMAN & LITTLEFIELD PUBLISHERS, INC.
Lanham • Boulder • New York • Toronto • Plymouth, UK

Published by Lexington Books
A division of Rowman & Littlefield Publishers, Inc.
A wholly owned subsidiary of The Rowman & Littlefield Publishing Group, Inc.
4501 Forbes Boulevard, Suite 200, Lanham, Maryland 20706
http://www.lexingtonbooks.com

Estover Road, Plymouth PL6 7PY, United Kingdom

British Library Cataloguing in Publication Information Available

Library of Congress Cataloging-in-Publication Data

Miccoli, Anthony, 1972–
  Posthuman suffering and the technological embrace / Anthony Miccoli.
    p. cm.
  Includes bibliographical references (p.   ) and index.
  ISBN 978-0-7391-2633-2 (cloth : alk. paper)
  ISBN 978-0-7391-4402-2 (electronic)
  1. Technology—Philosophy. 2. Human body—Technological innovations. 3. Cyborgs.
4. Humanism. 5. Suffering. 6. Artificial intelligence—Social aspects. 7. Philosophical
anthropology. I. Title.
  T14.5.M52 2009
  128—dc22   2009038848

Printed in the United States of America

For Alina—"the voice of your eyes is deeper than all roses"

And in loving memory of
Joseph & Rina D'Angieri
and
Carolyn Miccoli

Contents

Preface

Technic Excavations

One of the greatest difficulties in writing any theoretical treatment of technology is the fact that time is against you. The place one chooses to plant one's "post" is almost immediately subsumed by the tide of those who come after, rendering even the most prescient insights moot or obsolete in the time it takes for a manuscript to go to press. Revisions become a dual process: excavating the texts that were lost in the debris of composition, while simultaneously erecting statements on the very ground being excavated. As this text evolved from its earliest stages as a doctoral dissertation to its present form, I found myself guilty of the same shortcoming of which I had been so quick to accuse Hayles and Haraway: using discourse in an attempt to shore up the constantly shifting ontological ground.

Mark B. N. Hansen, one of the authors I "excavated" late in the process, so accurately points to this very occurrence, calling out the *technesis* of technology theorists who are so tempted to cling to a poststructuralist movement of deconstruction, that they lose sight of their own logocentric maneuvers.[1] We can hardly blame them. We investigate the implications of technology using the technology at hand: discourse. In order to "embrace" we must first define and instantiate the concept at the edges, and define "technology" in such a way that the act of definition becomes invisible. Hayles, Haraway, Freud, Heidegger, and Lyotard all struggle in their own ways to either directly or indirectly "work through" their own technological definitions, attempting to erect solid discursive structures on constantly shifting ground.

In that way, this text is no different. "Technology" becomes a placeholder, conceptually taking the shape of the discourse that attempts to define it (thus, I can even justify the previous deflection: technology = discourse.[2] However, it is in that very act of placeholding that we can, perhaps, make inroads. My subsequent treatments of Hayles and Haraway have proven accurate, especially in light of each author's more recent texts. In Hayles' *My Mother Was a Computer*, she references her earlier work and states that "the interplay between the liberal humanist subject and the posthuman that I used to launch my analysis . . . has already begun to fade into the history of the twentieth century"; that "new and more sophisticated versions of the posthuman have evolved."[3] Indeed it has, but "the Posthuman version 2.x" still *represents* the same lack that its predecessor did. Furthermore, by abandoning her earlier investigation of the "interplay between The liberal humanist subject and the posthuman," and instead shifting her focus to narrative and textuality, Hayles falls deeper into the logocentric trap which Hansen points out. By no means does this undermine the value or validity of Hayles' work; quite the contrary: her trajectory continues to define the leading edge of posthumanist discourse.

In regard to Haraway, her problematic tendency in her earlier work to elevate the "cyborg" as an ethereal, almost transcendent "other" becomes even more apparent in her later text, *Modest_Witness*. There, cyborgs have become even more abstract, described as: "offspring of technoscientific wombs," "imploded germinal entities," "densely packed condensations of worlds," and, perhaps most indulgently, brought into being by the "force of the implosion of the natural and artificial, subject and object, machine and organic body, money and lives, narrative and reality."[4] The difficulty here is that any attempt to excavate the assumptions behind these abstractions itself becomes a manifestation of liberal humanist domination, even though Haraway herself states that "Cyborg figures must be read, too, with . . . mixed, unfinished literacies."[5] This too becomes an act of *technesis*: cyborgs are figures (texts) to be read, privileging the *logos*, the heart of the very liberal humanism which Haraway erects the Cyborg to subvert.

Even in light of more recent posthumanist discourse, the claims which follow remain the same: That the "posthuman," in most posthumanist rhetoric, is a rearticulation—rather than a critique—of the liberal humanist subject. While this conclusion is supported by Hansen in *Embodying Technesis* via an investigation of the metaphorical shifts in posthumanist discourse, *Posthuman Suffering* arrives at this idea by investigating the *actual* interface between "the human" and "technology." By using Elaine Scarry's *The Body in Pain*, I address the question of how and why technology is, in Hansen's view, so easily "put into discourse." The answer is found, paradoxically, in the "lifting out" and "outsourcing" of pain that I outline in chapter one: the posthuman becomes "a means to substantiate and anthropomorphize the technological other into something that can be embraced (and embrace back) in light of the 'building out' of skill which characterizes technological development." Hansen's "putting-into-discourse" (technesis) becomes the "embracing back" which I articulate using examples from literature and film.

In addition to literary and filmic examples, I feel that it is also important to include, for lack of a better term, more "mundane" manifestations of technology itself. Indeed, psychopharmacology, artificial intelligence, and artificial life research are very relevant to an ongoing investigation of posthumanity (and much has been written about them),[6] but it is in these more "mundane" technological artifacts that the trauma of the "lifting out" or "outsourcing" of human efficacy most clearly takes place. Posthuman suffering is not only a theoretical issue, it happens on a daily basis, to "regular" people. As I outline in chapter two of *Posthuman Suffering* using the very simple example of a broken pencil point, our human agency is brought into question when we experience technological failures. We subconsciously (and traumatically) cede power to our technological artifacts, and are further traumatized when those artifacts fail. The flashes of anger that wash over us when the most simple tool fails; the feeling of abject terror that occurs when a doctoral student's laptop crashes mid-dissertation; or even the "pride" we feel when we see "all four bars" on our cell phones—all of these are manifestations of the "technological embrace."

This leads to my choice of Elaine Scarry's *The Body in Pain* as the thread holding the overall discussion together. I am asking my readers to become critically aware of their own uses of technology, and how those technological artifacts simultaneously augment and diminish our agency—not simply theoretically—but actually, in the "real world." Hayles, Haraway, Heidegger, Lyotard, consistently evade these discussions by conjuring up theoretical transcendent beings, scenarios, and vagaries which only push discussion of posthumanism deeper into abstraction. Pain is visceral, more visceral than pleasure, language, art, or "technesis." Scarry's contention that technological artifacts are "expressions" of pain provide *the* rhetorical backbone of the text, and make possible my own contention that we create technological artifacts so that the "lifeworld" (a dubious term at best) can suffer with us. It is this desire which recursively affects the founding notions of posthuman theory, causing its overall failure to negotiate the nature of the boundary between the "human" and the "technological." As a result of this failure, posthumanism alienates itself from broader theoretical, psychological, and practical ramifications of our perceived relationship to a technological "other." Thus, the following chapters are necessarily a treatment of *the* foundational texts of posthumanism, and become the mark of an attempt to establish some stability on ever-shifting ground.

Notes

1. See Mark Hansen, *Embodying Technisis: Technology Beyond Writing* (Ann Arbor, MI: The University of Michigan Press, 2000), specifically his introduction for his discussion of "Technostudies."

2. If we adhere to a traditional concept of "technology" using the Greek *tekhne* as a basis, then the term implies an art, skill, craft, or system, thus leading to *tekhnologia* referring to a "systematic treatment of an art, craft, or technique." *Online Etymology Dictionary,* s.v. "Technology," http://etymonline.com.

3. N. Katherine Hayles, *My Mother Was A Computer: Digital Subjects and Literary Texts* (Chicago: The University of Chicago Press, 1999), 2.

4. Donna M. Haraway. *Modest Witness@Second_Millenium.FemaleMan©_Meets_OncoMouse™: Feminism and Technoscience* (New York: Routledge, 1997), 14.

5. Haraway, *Modest_Witness,* 14.

6. For a broad range of articles regarding the various aspects of posthumanism, see *Cultural Critique* 53 (Winter 2003).

Acknowledgments

Many thanks go to Jeffrey Berman, Bret Benjamin, and Helen Elam who showed support, guidance, and patience during my doctoral work at the State University of New York at Albany; and to Bret Benjamin especially who often supplied me with faith in this project when my own temporarily ran out. I would also like to thank my colleagues at Western State College of Colorado who supported me through the publication process, especially John Hausdoerffer, who provided constant encouragement during the revision process. I owe a great deal to Nancy Gauss and Patrick Muckleroy of the Savage Library at Western State College for their help in tracking down hard-to-find material. Thanks also to my editor Joseph Parry and Editorial Assistant Jana Wilson from Lexington for their support and guidance, and to John Zuern for his invaluable comments on the manuscript. I am also grateful to the Center for Teaching Excellence at Western State College of Colorado for their grant and its partial support of permissions costs.

Thanks to those who granted permission to reprint excerpts from their work: from *White Noise* by Don DeLillo, copyright © 1984, 1985 by Don DeLillo. Used by permission of Viking Penguin, a division of Penguin Group (USA) Inc.; from *The Crying of Lot 49* by Thomas Pynchon, copyright © 1965 by Thomas Pynchon, copyright renewed 1993, 1994 by Thomas Pynchon. Reprinted by permission of HarperCollins Publishers; from *The Body in Pain: The Making and Unmaking of the World* by Elaine Scarry, copyright © 1985 by Elaine Scarry. Used by permission of Oxford University Press, Inc.

I am also indebted to Joyce DeWitt-Parker. Words cannot express my thanks for her insight and understanding. I am confident that I would not be where I am today if it were not for her guidance and assistance. Thanks also to Dr. Pam vonMatthiessen and Dr. Anthony Timko, who saved this book by saving my life. I also want to thank my parents, Charles and Laurette Miccoli, for trusting my decisions as I embarked upon my career.

Finally, deepest and most profound thanks to my wife and colleague, Alina M. Luna. Your unwavering faith in me, your patience, devotion, and insights (both intellectual and emotional) pulled me through the darkest times. None of this would have been possible without you.

Introduction

Posthuman Assumptions and the Technological Embrace

The presence of . . . man made implants and mechanisms within the body does not compromise or "dehumanize" a creature who has always located his or her humanity in self-artifice. If we do not yet have the descriptive mechanism that can account for the way in which human beings unconsciously assumed responsibility for their own bodily evolution, evolution has at least brought us to a place where that unconscious goal, buried and inarticulate at our beginnings has finally surfaced and become indisputable.

—Elaine Scarry[1]

In the space between the "post" and "humanism" lies a conflict that plays itself out repeatedly in posthumanist discourse. Is posthumanism simply a continuation of liberal humanism—a "humanism 2.0"—re-cast in terms of technology and contemporary theories of information, allowing for the consciousness to be lifted out and uploaded into a machine? Or is posthumanism truly a new field of inquiry re-evaluating humanism itself, questioning the viability, desirability, and expression of the Cartesian self in light of humanity's technological advancements? A third possibility also arises: is posthumanism an epistemology unto itself; a way in which we choose to orient ourselves, to literally apprehend, the world? Or could posthumanism be the very "descriptive mechanism" which Elaine Scarry, writing in 1985, identifies—a discourse that explores technology as a human expression of suffering and pain?

In order to engage these questions, we must first explore the history of posthumanism, specifically through the work of one of the major voices in posthuman theory. N. Katherine Hayles is consistently cited as a pioneer of the field, and perhaps *the* most influential voice in critical posthumanism.[2] While Hayles puts forth a call to avoid being drawn in by romanticized, science-fiction scenarios of mind uploading and human/machine hybrids, her work (and as we will see, those who came before and after) still suffers from unsuccessful attempts to negotiate the nature of the boundary between human and machine. These difficulties eventually constitute the space between the "post-" and the "human."

According to Hayles, the posthuman is characterized by four main points, all of which are still at work in current posthumanist discourse. The first is the privileging of "informational pattern over material instantiation."[3] Information is viewed "not as an object but as a resultant measurement from processes, and each of these processes is a differential between some two values."[4] As Hayles

1

is fond of saying, "information lost its body." In *How We Became Posthuman,* she pinpoints this shift occurring in the years following World War II.[5]

What warrants further study (and will be discussed in later chapters) is that although the field of cybernetics may have been born in the postwar era, the reframing of information—especially in relation to the concept of the human "self," can also be traced back to Freudian psychoanalysis.[6] What is most important at the present moment, however, is the fact that posthumanism in *all* of its manifestations, relies on the assumption that information can be freely passed from one substrate to another.[7]

Following this reconceptualization of information, we come to the second aspect of the posthuman view: The body is a prosthesis for consciousness, characterized as more of a tool that can be improved, reconfigured, and quite possibly shed for a better one. The body also becomes temporary, not simply because it will eventually die, but temporary in terms of human evolution. Humanity will (and must) eventually evolve beyond its body into a possibly—but not necessarily—artificial, technological manifestation. Consciousness would become fully transferable. Biological embodiment is considered a chance event in our evolution rather than as an inevitable condition of life.

Thirdly, the posthuman view "considers consciousness . . . as an epiphenomenon."[8] Consciousness is not the *defining* characteristic of humanity. Rather, it is a result of our ongoing evolution. In its more pessimistic connotations, consciousness is viewed as an evolutionary necessity, a centralized and overlying *informational* control system by which the complex functions of the body are maintained. One of the inherent ironies of posthumanism has its roots here. The "epiphenomenon" of consciousness—while often de-emphasized in relation to other biological processes of the body, does indeed become the star of the show, so to speak, as the very aspect of our human "selves" that theoretically could be uploaded into a machine. In fact, the one consistency among different applications of posthumanism is the ongoing metaphorical objectification of the consciousness as some-thing which can be moved, relocated, downloaded, uploaded, or otherwise lifted out of the human.[9]

Finally and most importantly, the posthuman view reconceptualizes the human being so that it can be better articulated—made more compatible—with computerized systems or possible artificial intelligences. According to Hayles, the posthuman is most accurately characterized by the idea that there are no "essential differences or absolute demarcations between bodily existence and computer simulation, cybernetic mechanisms and biological organism, robot teleology and human goals."[10] In this regard, all aspects of human biological functioning—including consciousness—are considered in terms of informational processes. Ultimately, the "self" is no longer defined by its biological roots, but is instead characterized as a unique pattern of information.

In four steps, the human being is broken down into a technological metaphor, more easily integrated with contemporary theories of information and information processing. Furthermore, this "datafied" human is now governed by the same rules and judged by the same qualities as artificial, information-processing device: how *compatible* is it with its environment, with others, with itself? How well does it interface with information? Those questions become even more important when we consider compatibility itself by its purest etymological roots in the term *compassion*—literally "to suffer together."[11] While in recent years posthuman theory has been more receptive to exploring the epistemological and ontological aspects of the relationship between humanity and technology, the site of interface between the two still eludes broader critical inquiry. The nature of this interface (i.e., its topography, its cognitive implications), and how the relationship between "human" and "technological" subjects play out in the "lifeworld" becomes a significant space for critical investigation. To better negotiate this space, I choose the lead of Elaine Scarry's *The Body in Pain: The Making and Unmaking of the World* to help explore and articulate that site of interface.

Before we can advance, it is necessary to attempt to nail down the term "technology" itself. One of the first traps we can avoid is equivocating what technology *is* with what technology *means*. For the purposes of the present study, technology is defined as the external manifestation of artifice, methodology, or skill, and the systems of use of any combination thereof.

Disembodying the Subject: The Human and the Post

What makes *How We Became Posthuman* most important is that it is one of the first attempts to look at the posthuman in a historical and critical fashion. *How We Became Posthuman* is a parallel text, tracing a history of what Hayles views as a disembodiment of information as "an entity separate from the material forms in which it is thought to be embedded"[12] while also investigating what she perceives as an ongoing temptation to re-articulate the disembodied liberal humanist subject in more technologically compatible terms.[13]

While Hayles repeatedly calls for a more critical posthumanism which freely takes into account (and even celebrates) the uniqueness of human physiological/biological embodiment, *How We Became Posthuman* generally works under the assumption that a human being's true potential can only be reached through technology. Furthermore, the quality of our posthuman existence is best improved through a more comprehensive understanding of not only the technological systems with which we work every day, but also with the information which defines both human and technological systems themselves. The difficulty here is that Hayles inadvertently implies that the quality of our lives is directly proportional to the degree and quality of our compatibility with information.

As Hayles systematically presents the ongoing disembodiment of information from the late 1940s, she also points out a "piecing apart" of the self, showing how the liberal humanist subject has remained privileged by re-casting the physical body (and consequently the human brain) as nothing more than an organic information-processing device. The reconceptualization of information as a free-floating entity which can be transmitted seamlessly from one substrate to another (i.e. from silicon-based electronic components to carbon-based organic components) makes it much easier to downplay the "materiality in which the thinking mind is instantiated."[14]

If—in the coldest of posthuman interpretations—human thought was nothing more than a form of information processing, then, theoretically, it could be *directly* transferred or uploaded to a computer, which could then process that same information, just in a different form. Human cognition—the mark of the Cartesian self—becomes simply(!) an interplay of patterns of information. The self-as-information, in Hayles' view, has the potential to become just another reinscription of the liberal humanist subject, especially in light of its own self-awareness. As long as the "pattern" of self-awareness is present, the self exists.

This reinscription, however, is exactly what Hayles believes Posthumanism should investigate and deconstruct (thus the birth of a more formal "critical posthumanism"). By divesting information of its materiality, we run the risk of "rewriting" the same disembodiment which is implied in liberal humanism onto contemporary, technologically-influenced notions of subjectivity.[15] Posthumanism, for Hayles, is not the means by which we jettison our bodies in order to insert our "selves" into the machine. Instead, it becomes a means by which we critically "re-flesh" the self in light of our ongoing and accelerating technological development. Note Hayles' self-proclaimed posthuman "dream":

> my dream is a version of the posthuman that embraces the possibilities of information technologies without being seduced by fantasies of unlimited power and disembodied immortality, that recognizes and celebrates finitude as a condition of human being, and that understands human life is embedded in a material world of great complexity, one on which we depend for our continued survival.[16]

The willful embracing of technology is an important image to retain, since it implies a taking in or enclosing: it is better for the human to take in technology than to have technology take in (or perhaps overtake) the human. But Hayles (and others) fails to address the irony of the image itself: the act of an embrace *necessitates* the existence of a unified, liberal humanist subject. While the image may seem almost nurturing, an embrace is also a means of *control*, which might explain why the opposite image—the machine embracing the human—is portrayed as a perverse nightmare. The personification of the posthuman as an entity which can "recognize" and "understand" recursively facilitates the projection of those human qualities onto technological systems themselves, especially if the posthuman is embedded fully into the technological systems which surround it. Thus, this projection of human subjectivity and even human teleology can become so convincing that they seem to originate from the technological system itself.

It is also interesting to note what aspects Hayles uses to define the human. Finitude, materiality, and the *understanding of the complexity of the material world* are paramount not only to being human, but to our survival.[17] Posthumanism assumes that our survival depends on our ability to process information which does not necessarily imply *understanding* information. Unfortunately, the two terms are often equated in posthumanism, causing some of the deep-rooted contradictions which we will be examining here.

The linking of finitude to the image of the embrace is also telling, in that the embrace here seems to bring about a *conclusion* through a human enclosing of the technological other. In this regard, posthumanism becomes an artificial and imposed conclusion of humanism (and perhaps humanity) itself; the implication being that if we understand the relationship well enough, it will also bring about some kind of conclusion. The danger here is to confuse the idea of a conclusion (literally, an enclosing) with the idea of *completion* (literally, a filling up).[18] In posthumanism it becomes too easy to erroneously equate a "complete" (i.e. self-actualized, repression-free) human with the more accurate "concluded" one—the human who invokes the posthuman as a means to describe his or her belief that the supplement of technology brings them an expanded, more accurate self-awareness.

Hayles' characterization of what it means to be human becomes even more interesting when we look at her contrasting, posthuman "nightmare," which consists of: "a culture of posthumans who regard their bodies as fashion accessories rather than the ground of being."[19] It would seem that if we willfully embrace the complexity of technology, then we will—by default—embrace the "specialness" of our physicality. The "good posthuman" for Hayles is the critical posthuman who does not accept *carte blanche* the Cartesian self and its preponderance to privilege white, Western, male agendas,[20] but who maintains a recognition of his/her own relationship to—and reliance upon—technology. This reliance becomes an acceptable and necessary component to being a successful posthuman.[21]

Hayles emphasizes that posthumanism in and of itself is not dangerous: "what is lethal is not the posthuman as such, but the *grafting* of the posthuman onto *a liberal humanist view of the self*."[22] Grafting here stands as a stark contrast to the embrace mentioned earlier. The term brings to mind visions of Frankenstein-like cyborgs where mechanical parts protrude from (but more importantly, pierce into) human flesh. But again we must be aware of the metaphors Hayles employs. This critical, seemingly benevolent posthumanism is something that characterizes technology as graspable, embraceable—images that empower the human, as opposed to the nightmare images of grafting and (as we will later see with Haraway) insertion. But even the positive imagery used still implies the human as necessarily *separate* from the technology he or she is reaching for. In fact, to be a successful posthuman, we must be cognizant of the boundary at all times. The Cartesian self/other dichotomy still remains in control.

This is where the prospect of posthumanism gets complicated. This is also where we can see the beginnings of the "suffering" that is present in posthumanism itself. We have to be aware of the boundaries between human and machine, but only to subvert them. Eschewing the flesh altogether, by Hayles' standards, implies ignorance; the possible transferring of the consciousness into a machine does not represent an abandoning of the liberal humanist subject, but simply means that the subject is "expanding its prerogatives."[23] Instead of subverting boundaries, expanding the self moves those boundaries further out into the material world, re-erecting them between what is self and not-self, and, most importantly, "authoriz[ing] the fear that if the boundaries are breached at all, there will be nothing to stop the self's complete dissolution."[24] Also, in the simplest of terms, expanding the prerogatives of the self also implies that, if the self is composed of information, an expanded self would consist of more information of which to keep track.

For Hayles, uploading the consciousness—"datafying" the self—might grant us immortality, but it will not ease the Cartesian fear of annihilation. Ironically, it would serve only to increase those fears.[25] Significantly, all of this has been carried out in Hayles' text without a direct discussion of Cartesian humanism. It is as if the fact that we have "already become posthuman"[26] makes the detailed discussion of humanism a moot point, inserting an arbitrary—if not convenient—conclusion to humanism.

So, a good posthuman is, literally, a knowing and informed posthuman, who realizes that the human self is *not* autonomous, and is not defined by unambiguous boundaries.[27] The boundary between real and virtual[28] is permeable, and the technologies that help traverse that boundary can be fully utilized only when we understand how much the *body* matters. For Hayles, the human self, as an embodied entity, is unified and permeable, capable of figuratively and literally incorporating technological artifacts into itself while still self-consciously maintaining a boundary between them. What is at stake for posthumanism is *how* that incorporation takes place (or how the "self" is supposed to be expanded). By envisioning the human in such a way, in the posthuman model

> human functionality expands because the parameters of the cognitive system it inhabits expand. In this model, it is not a question of leaving the body behind but rather of extending embodied awareness in highly specific, local, and material ways that would be impossible without electronic prosthesis.[29]

However, this model sets up an entirely new fear and type of suffering—one that stems from our relationship (or lack thereof) with information. The desire to be distributed and permeable to information does not instantiate the ability to be distributed, nor does it bring with it the ability to understand that information. Thus, we are constantly faced with the notion that it is only through technological means that we can become fully human, and that the degree and quality of our humanity are defined by our relationship to our own information. For our cognitive systems to expand, we *must* be able to more efficiently understand *more* information.

Evaluating Hayles:
Finding Our "Selves" and the Responsibility of Evolution

I believe that Hayles' "informed posthuman" sets up a model for human being which is, at best, problematic. To "extend embodied awareness" is a difficult task, even without technological systems tempting us to cling more tenaciously to our (Cartesian) selves. Hayles also, inadvertently I think, sets up the potential for an internal conflict within posthumanism. There are two distinct movements at work in *How We Became Posthuman*. The first is a call for an embracing of technology—its artifacts, its systems, its possibilities, *and* its faults. She calls us to accept technology for what it is, not necessarily for what we can make it into; for doing so will cause us to seek out a dangerous desire for immortality and a mode of being which is unrealistic. It is this latter possibility which, in more extropian modes, holds the most potential to be forgotten as people attempt to apply posthumanist perspectives in scientific research.

The second movement is a more subtle call to assert our "selves"—not so much as to cut off the possibilities that an embracing of technology would bring us, but instead to be able to retain some kind of cohesive self-image that not only allows us to exist as fully embodied entities, but allows the "specialness" of our physical, human embodiment to be reflected in the technological systems which allow that embodiment to become fully realized. The key problem here is the assumption that complete *human* embodiment can only be attained through *technology*; being "informed" regarding the connection is equated with a true embrace of the systems through which we will attain a full embodiment—our completion.[30] Hayles calls for us to hang onto just enough self-image so that it can be projected onto (and into) our technological systems in order that it can be eventually reflected back to us.

Hayles is working under the assumption that true bodily "awareness" can come from *understanding* the body conceptually, as a system of processes—rather than viscerally, as biological entity which experiences pain and pleasure. Like Freud before her, Hayles seems to believe that an understanding of the processing of information will bring with it a sense of balance that will manifest itself in our physical well-being. Hayles' also seems to be equating the concept of full human embodiment with human *agency*, assuming that if we reach our fully embodied potential, then we can have a greater, more efficient effect on the world around us.

In order for us to reach our embodied potential, we would have to be as compatible—as in tune—as possible to the technological systems that posthumanism believes will help us reach that potential. The irony here is that in the strictest sense, when one system is fully compatible with another, there are no perceived operational differences between one system and the other. In human/machine terms, to achieve full compatibility, we would necessarily have to become *less aware* of the connection in order to use technology effectively.

Hayles' posthuman dream actually would require us to be unaware of our connection to technology in order to become aware of it.

The site of slippage in Hayles (and Posthumanism) comes at the point of interface itself. The fully posthuman individual would not dream of an awareness of his/her connection—his/her interface—to the machine, the posthuman would not dream of connection at all; because the *direct* connection to a technological system would be so intrinsic that the most basic self/other relationship would be non-existent. Hayles' post-human dream is just that—a dream; and a very liberal humanist one at that. It is a dream which can be perpetually aspired to but necessarily never achieved. If humanity were to achieve this connection, it would truly mark the end of *homo sapiens* and the beginning of a new species.

Taken to its ultimate conclusions, the posthuman dream points to a "transcendence" rather than embodied awareness, implying that the *need* for connection would eventually be erased, and that we would eventually evolve into a species that no longer relied on technology at all. What posthumanism avoids addressing is the very need for connection, as well as the site of interface where the connection takes place. Rather than deal directly with either of these issues, posthumanism precludes further discourse by invoking its status as being "already here." It chooses to begin *after* the connection has been made, and not more directly problematize the physical, emotional, and theoretical issues that the interface raises. Posthumanism contends that we are already posthuman. Why then are we constantly striving for better connections with our machines? Why so often, when we feel alienated from our technological systems—our tools, our cars, our computers—do we forgo traditional means of manipulation and interface? We speak to them, we "will them" work, we curse, we beg, we *pray*—often not to a specific deity, but *to the system itself*.

All too often, this is the aspect of the human/technological relationship that posthumanists tend to marginalize, dealing with it only anecdotally, in footnotes, or banished to a prologue or epilogue.[31] It is as if the visceral human—the human who bears pleasure and pain, the human who *feels*—is merely the physical expression of the more pure, more ethereal "datafied" human. Science may someday prove this incontrovertibly. But it is the visceral human that the post-human has yet to address. When we strip away all layers of technology, all objects that came to be through human artifice, we are left only with the human. Thus we must return to the human, and the human's most basic wants and needs, in order to understand the posthuman.

Elaine Scarry: Reconfiguring the Embrace

To understand the deeper implications of "embodiment" in light of posthumanism, we turn to Elaine Scarry's *The Body in Pain: The Making and Unmaking of the World*. In her book, Scarry centers the defining characteristic of humanity in the way in which human beings experience and express physical pain. Scarry's work anticipates more formal posthuman discourse through her characterization of human artifice (especially the development of more complex technological systems) as a means by which we extend our sense of awareness and make our "selves" available to others. However, Scarry's approach focuses specifically on the site of interface—where the individual human and the tool he or she uses—come together figuratively, metaphorically, *and* physically. It is this site of interface—the point of actual contact between human and machine—that posthumanism tends to avoid.

Where posthumanism attempts to understand the human through technology, Scarry's approach keeps the biological human in the foreground, portraying technological artifacts and their systems of use as a means of expression. All human-made artifacts, according to Scarry, are literal objectifications of specific needs, desires, and means of relieving pain; all are ways of making internal experience sharable with the world. As the scope of her study widens, she never loses sight of the uniqueness of the human physical response to pain, and the psychological means by which we make that pain available to others.

If we are to truly understand the human embrace of technology that posthumanism implies, if we are to—as Hayles poses—"re-flesh" our bodies and "make them matter" again, then we can only do so through an examination of the most basic reasons why we turn to technology at all. Most importantly, the ongoing discussion of Scarry's work will help us address the underlying expectations of technology implied in posthumanism itself.

For Scarry, pure, complete "embodiment" has a very different, less positive connotation than Hayles presents. Hayles' re-fleshed human is vastly improved through an extended awareness of the delineation between body and technological other. The fully-embodied posthuman achieves more agency in the world because of its effective manipulation of information and technological systems. Scarry's characterization of complete embodiment is, by contrast, a total *lack* of agency in the world. One's degree of embodiment depends upon the amount of physical pain from which one is suffering. Pain and suffering act to bring the body to the forefront, at the cost of the outside world; it is "a way of so emphasizing the body that the contents of the world are cancelled."[32] The greater the pain, the more inwardly focused we become.

Pain limits our agency in the world because of its certainty. Scarry states that "for the person in pain, so incontestably and unnegotiably present is that 'having pain' may come to be the most vibrant example of what is to 'have certainty.'"[33] While we may be able to indicate to others that we are in pain, we cannot effectively share the *certainty* of that pain. When we witness others in pain, we cannot *know* that same pain. It is not transferable, it can only be witnessed second-hand. For those that witness pain, "it is so elusive that 'hearing about pain' may exist as the primary model of what is 'to have doubt.'"[34] It becomes impossible to give that pain a voice.

Pain is not just language-defying, it is language-destroying; extreme pain "bring[s] about an immediate reversion to a state anterior to language, to the sounds and cries a human being makes before language is learned."[35] The experience of pain can be characterized specifically as *suffering* when there is *another* to bear witness to that pain.[36] For Scarry, it is this ability to witness other's pain—to have feelings for someone (or something) which becomes "a consistent affirmation of the human being's capacity to move out beyond the boundaries of his or her body into the external, sharable world."[37] And, in the most extreme instances of pain, when the person suffering is so fully embodied that he or she no longer has the capacity for language itself, the language of that pain is "brought into being by those who are not themselves in pain but who speak *on behalf* of those who are."[38] An intensely *internal* experience is expressed externally by an other. Pain can neither be confirmed nor denied.

Of course, the above model illustrates the most extreme, "language destroying" instances of pain. But when pain is not too intense as to fully curtail the ability to speak, the only way to share that pain (for sympathy, for relief, or for the eventual elimination of that pain) is to find some means of expressing it. Somehow, the pain must be objectified in order that it may be "knowable" to others, and "lifted into the visible world." Scarry further explains "*if the referent for these now objectified attributes is understood to be the human body*, then the sentient fact of the person's suffering will become knowable to a second person."[39]

Scarry's theory of pain and sentience becomes most pertinent to posthumanism, however, when she proposes that "the felt attributes of pain" can be "attached to a *referent other than the human body*"—a process she calls "analogical verification" or "analogical substantiation":

> the felt-characteristics of pain—one of which its compelling vibrancy or its incontestable reality or simply its "certainty"—can be appropriated away from the body and presented as the attributes of something else (something which by itself lacks those attributes, something which does not in itself appear vibrant, real, or certain).[40]

Scarry's ongoing articulation of the process by which we project human attributes onto non-human objects addresses a fundamental lack in posthuman discourse, where technological artifacts and systems are so often assumed (or expected) to extend the scope of human awareness and experience. While posthumanism may indirectly attempt to problematize this relationship, Scarry addresses the more basic reason *why* humans turn to material objects to "expand awareness" in the first place—we do so as a way to make ourselves "available" to others.[41]

For Scarry, technology is *not* a means to achieve some kind of improved embodiedness (e.g., Hayles), instead, it is a means by which "a bodily attribute is projected into the artifact (a fiction, a made thing) which essentially takes on the work of the body, thereby freeing the embodied person of discomfort and thus enabling him to enter a larger realm of self-extension."[42] Technology allows the internal to be expressed in the outside world. Even on the smallest scale, the tool—no matter how primitive or advanced—is the "concrete" and "palpable" surface across which "the interior act and exterior object become continuous."[43]

Posthumanism, in its zeal to conclude the human, portrays technology as an "other" to be embraced, and consequently has lost sight of the basic realities of human/technological interface. I believe that what lies at the heart of posthumanism is a desire for compatibility—not in terms of a streamlined, just-seamless-enough connection with technology—but in terms of a more literal "suffering together." In general, posthumanism looks to technology as a superior model of information processing to which humans aspire. Whether it is the most extreme extropian desire to upload the consciousness and forgo the body completely, or the more subtle, critical desire to understand the human in technological terms, both are looking to re-articulate the human (one literally, the other figuratively) *in terms* of technology.

In the rush to explain the "how," posthumanism does not fully engage the "why." I believe that we want the technological systems around us—on a most fundamental level—to suffer with us. We want, as Scarry says "to deprive the external world of the privilege of being inanimate."[44] We do not embrace technology to expand our selves, we embrace technology so that *it may embrace us*, suffer with us, and become that elusive *created* other whose exclusive purpose it is to perfectly articulate—and express—our suffering for us.

We are looking to our machines to speak, feel, experience on behalf of us—to be the technological other to perfectly bear witness to our own pain. Posthumanist discourse, in its attempts to engage the human *in terms of* the technological, often takes an "either/or" approach—leaning hard on the liberal humanist subject (despite its own calls *not* to do so) and characterizes technology as a distinct other than can only be rendered indistinct once it has been properly (and knowingly) embraced.

Posthumanist discourse also views embodiment only in terms of cognition, seeing the human as only an embodied mind, rather than—for lack of a better phrase—a *mindful body.* By not taking into consideration even the most basic of human sensory experiences, posthumanism unwittingly alienates the very body which Hayles believes it should "re-flesh."[45]

If we were to follow Hayles' initial call to re-flesh ourselves, becoming more centered in our physicality, we would run the risk of becoming less connected to others and find ourselves more apt to rely on artifice—the use and creation of technological tools and the "marks" they make—to re-establish connections with the world around us. In short, the more embodied we are, the greater the need to move outward and seek means of expression.

It is my belief that posthumanism potentially alienates itself from the broader ramifications—theoretical, psychological, and practical—of the complex network of relationships between humans and the technological "other." Most specifically, posthumanism has the potential to address what I believe is a growing compulsive relationship with technology, where technological systems become the target for externalized expressions of technologically-induced obsessive/compulsive symptoms. We "surf the net," e-mail, and instant message avowedly as a means of communication and connection with others, when in reality we are often doing so as a means to sublimate the deeper traumas that those very technological systems bring about and eventually exacerbate.

The Approach

In order to effectively deal with such a wide range of issues across so many different "registers," it will be necessary to strip away the levels of abstraction which have distanced us from the true nature of the human/technological relationship. So far, Hayles has provided us with a viable framework of the "present history" of posthumanism. With the "post" firmly planted, Scarry supplies us with the "human"—a parallel path which will run continuously through different layers that will be peeled back as we progress.

Donna Haraway's "Cyborg Manifesto" will provide us with the foundations that inspired Hayles through an insightful anticipation of the posthuman, characterized by a very anthropomorphic "Cyborg" which seeks a human embrace. Beyond Haraway, we will delve into the more theoretical waters of Heidegger's "Question Concerning Technology," and Lyotard's "Inhuman." That section will necessarily re-situate technology not as an other to be embraced, but as a means for humans to embrace the world. With those layers carefully cleared, the submerged connection between posthumanism and Freudian psychoanalytic theory will be exposed. Not only does posthumanism place the technological as a model to which we aspire (as Freud did in the technological idiom of his time), but posthumanism also has difficulty rectifying the idea of a "concluded" human with a "completed" one (a difficulty Freud attempted to deal with in "Analysis Terminable and Interminable"). Achieving a true "posthumanist" state is as elusive (if not impossible) as attaining the true psychoanalytic "cure."

The literary texts I have included serve the singular purpose of providing viable examples of the impossibility of true human/technological interface that posthumanism tempts us to idolize. For Oedipa Maas in *The Crying of Lot 49*, Jack Gladney in *White Noise,* and most directly Monica Swinton in the film *A.I. Artificial Intelligence,* each seeks out a direct—interface-less—connection to what they consider to be their *defining* technological systems. All of them feel inadequate in relation to the technological systems in which they have placed their faith. Their prayer-like interactions, and at times, pleadings, with those systems are dramatic representations of the same pleadings we perform every day when we empower our machines.

Notes

1. Elaine Scarry, *The Body in Pain: The Making and Unmaking of the World* (New York: Oxford University Press, 1985), 253-4.

2. Eugene Thacker identifies two main movements within contemporary posthumanist discourse. The first of which, "extropianism . . . includes theoretical-technical inquiries into the next phase of the human condition through advances in science and technology. These are mostly technophilic accounts of the radical changes that leading-edge technology will bring." The second he identifies as "critical posthumanism," which is characterizes as "being a response to [extropianism]" and attempts to "[bring] together the implications of postmodern theories of the subject and the politics of new technologies." Eugene Thacker, "Data Made Flesh: Biotechnology and the Discourse of the Posthuman," *Cultural Critique* 53 (2003): 72-97.

3. N. Katherine Hayles, *How We Became Posthuman: Virtual Bodies in Cybernetics, Literature, and Informatics* (Chicago: The University of Chicago Press, 1999), 2.

4. Thacker, "Data Made Flesh," 82.

5. In the years following World War II, the "cyborg" became an increasingly dominant technological artifact and cultural icon. Cybernetics itself was a comparative study of control processes in mechanical, biological, and electronic systems, and an ongoing field of inquiry as to the similarities of these processes in biological and artificial systems. At the forefront of cybernetics were John Van Neumann, Claude Shannon, and Warren McCulloch, among others. From 1943 to 1954, these scientists held a series of meetings, collectively known as "The Macy Conferences" which attempted to put forth new theories of information, and new information-processing models of neural functioning. The resulting cybernetic paradigm, as Hayles puts it, was "nothing less than a new way of looking at human beings. Henceforth, humans were to be seen primarily as information-processing entities who are *essentially* similar to intelligent machines." Hayles, *Posthuman*, 7 (emphasis hers).

6. More specifically, Freudian psychoanalysis implies that traumatic events act as sources of psychological/mental pressure or energy. The events we experience become "quantified" as information with a substantive quality, which often had physical effects as psychosomatic symptoms. Through psychoanalysis, those symptoms can be alleviated via the proper interpretation of information.

7. It is crucial to keep in mind that in Wiener's and Shannon's theories, information had to be decontextualized in order for it to maintain its integrity across different substrates. "Shannon and Wiener defined information so that it would be calculated as the same value regardless of the contexts in which it was embedded, which is to say, they divorced it from meaning. *In context*, the definition allowed information to be conceptualized as if it were an entity that could flow unchanged between different material substrates, as when Moravec envisions the information contained in a brain being downloaded into a computer" Hayles, *Posthuman*, 54 (emphasis hers).

8. Hayles, *Posthuman*, 2.

9. Making the consciousness the *defining* characteristic of humanity runs the risk of downgrading the importance of the very embodiment of consciousness, and how the consciousness acts as a kind of "proprietary software" unique to our physical bodies. While Hayles calls directly for a more conscientious effort to emphasize this very point, posthumanism in general has trouble coming to terms with the realities of the embodied consciousness.

10. Hayles, *Posthuman*, 3.

11. Compassion: 1340, from O.Fr. *compassion*, from L.L. *compassionem* (nom. *compassio*) "sympathy," from *compassus*, pp. of *compati* "to feel pity," from *com-* "together" + *pati* "to suffer." Loan-translation of Gk. *sympatheia*. *Online Etylmology Dictionary*.

12. Hayles, *Posthuman*, 2.

13. It is important to understand that Hayles' choice to postpone a detailed discussion of the Cartesian subject in favor of an articulation of information theory is somewhat characteristic of posthuman discourse in general. The humanist subject is most often considered only as an entity which may or may not be "reinscribed" in light of technological development. I have deferred a more detailed discussion of Cartesian humanism in order to emphasize the implications of choosing to portray the technological "post" of posthumanism before humanism itself.

14. Hayles, *Posthuman*, 2.

15. Hayles, *Posthuman*, 5.

16. Hayles, *Posthuman*, 5.

17. This linking of understanding to survival will become an integral aspect of chapter 3's discussion of Jean-Francois Lyotard.

18. conclude: c.1300, from L. *concludere* "to shut up, enclose," from *com-* "together" + *-cludere*, comb. form of *claudere* "to shut." Compare that with complete: c.1384, from O.Fr. *complet* "full," from L. *completus*, pp. of *complere* "to fill up," from *com-* intensive prefix + *plere* "to fill." *Online Etymology Dictionary*.

19. Hayles, *Posthuman*, 5.

20. "Although I think that serious consideration needs to be given to how certain characteristics associated with the liberal subject, especially agency and choice, can be articulated within a posthuman context, I do not mourn the passing of a concept so deeply entwined with projects of domination and oppression." Hayles, *Posthuman*, 45. Hayles reiterates this opinion later when she discusses Haraway's "A Manifesto for Cyborgs: Science Technology, and Socialist Feminism in the 1980s." However, I will be discussing this in more detail in later chapters.

21. Hayles' Posthumanism has built into it a certain fear of commodification and obsolescence that are becoming increasingly predominant in Western—particularly American—society. We often find ourselves throwing away our "old" computers, cell phones, PDAs not because they don't function, but because they are no longer compatible with the operating systems and software needed to run them.

22. Hayles, *Posthuman*, 286 (emphasis mine).

23. Hayles, *Posthuman*, 287.

24. Hayles, *Posthuman*, 290.

25. In practical terms, a "datafied" self has the potential to be as susceptible to accidental deletion and/or corruption as a document on our hard drives.

26. Hayles, *Posthuman*, xiv.

27. Hayles, *Posthuman*, 291.

28. Hayles offers what she calls a "strategic definition" for virtuality: "*Virtuality is the cultural perception that material objects are interpenetrated by information patterns.* The definition plays off the duality at the heart of the condition of virtuality—materiality on one hand, information on the other." Hayles, *Posthuman*, 13-14 (emphasis hers).

29. Hayles, *Posthuman*, 290-91.

30. A very simple example of this pattern can be found in the film *WALL-E*. Humanity has collectively forgotten its potential due to its blind use of technology. Over-indulgent and over-stimulated humans simply drift on an intergalactic ocean liner. Humanity, however, rediscovers its purpose and becomes "more human" when humanized

machines such as WALL-E and EVE remind the humans how to live. The robots have retained some aspect of human teleology while the humans have forgotten it. However, when humans are in need of it again, it is easily re-acquired from the machines. Humans have "outsourced" their humanity to robots.

31. More often than not, when these basic issues of embodiment arise, critical posthumanism will turn to literary texts to "safely" articulate the more psychological, visceral consequences that manifest themselves when the relationship between human and machine is called into question.

32. Scarry, *The Body in Pain*, 34.

33. Scarry, *The Body in Pain*, 4.

34. Scarry, *The Body in Pain*, 4. It is important to note here that the "doubt" Scarry speaks of is not exactly a doubting of the *validity* of an expression of pain. Instead, it is a less tangible, more abstract doubt. One that is better characterized as the difference between believing something (i.e., having faith in something), and being *certain* of something—being able to prove something's presence or existence in an uncontestable way. Although we can witness a loved one in extreme pain, and it can overwhelmingly affect us emotionally (and perhaps even psychosomatically), we cannot share that particular pain. Even if we were to eventually suffer the same injury or illness, that pain would be uniquely ours.

35. Scarry, *The Body in Pain*, 4.

36. As we shall see, that "other" doesn't necessarily have to be human.

37. Scarry, *The Body in Pain*, 5.

38. Scarry, *The Body in Pain*, 6 (emphasis hers).

39. Scarry, *The Body in Pain*, 13 (emphasis hers).

40. Scarry, *The Body in Pain*, 14.

41. Scarry, *The Body in Pain*, 22.

42. Scarry, *The Body in Pain*, 144.

43. Scarry, *The Body in Pain*, 176.

44. Scarry, *The Body in Pain*, 285.

45. When Hayles calls for a greater embodiment, one can assume that she is not calling for us to experience more pain. However, if we follow Scarry's model, then any increased awareness of our bodies comes at the price of our awareness to our connection with our tools. Hayles attempts to work around this by sidestepping the visceral and locating "awareness" in the realm of the intellectual, a maneuver which requires at least some reinscription of the liberal humanist subject in order to work.

Chapter One

Inside Out and Prayers for Recognition:
Donna Haraway's "Cyborg Manifesto"
and
Thomas Pynchon's *The Crying of Lot 49*

> But to have no body is to have no limits on one's extension out into the world; conversely, to have a body, a body made emphatic by being continually altered through various forms of creation, instruction . . . and wounding, is to have one's sphere of extension contracted down to the small circle of one's immediate physical presence. Consequently to be extensively embodied is the equivalent of being unrepresented and (here as in many secular contexts) is almost always the condition of being without power.
>
> —Elaine Scarry[1]

For N. Katherine Hayles, we *are* posthuman, and the posthuman should be an informed balance of technology and biology in which technology allows us to achieve the potential of our bodies. Posthumanism effectively flips the technological/human relationship by assuming the superiority of the technological other, and using it as a model to which humans should aspire.

While Hayles goes to great lengths to "re-flesh" the human within posthuman discourse, she does so apologetically. Asking us to "celebrate finitude as a condition of human being."[2] Note that the *biological* certainty of our physicality is the conditional aspect of our humanity, and that it is technology that has the power to "seduce" us with "fantasies of unlimited power."[3] I find it most interesting that Hayles—and posthumanism in general—consistently empowers technology with such human attributes: technology tempts us with the datafied fruit of knowledge. But like Adam and Eve, taking a bite only makes us *more aware* of our nakedness and mortality.

My choice of religious metaphor here is far from arbitrary. As we move backward from *How We Became Posthuman* and descend more deeply into *The Body in Pain*, we'll see that the posthuman characterization of the human relationship with technology can be viewed in terms of an act of faith. We can trace the seemingly transcendent quality of the anthropomorphic posthuman presented by Hayles back to its precursor: Donna Haraway's cyborg, presented in her "Cyborg Manifesto: Science, Technology and Socialist-Feminism in the Late Twentieth Century." Haraway's portrayals of the cyborg shift from a blasphemous, bastard-child sprung from the highly anthropomorphic, to an amorphous, ethereal being that is actually *us*.

Donna Haraway and Blasphemous Cyborgs

There can be no discussion of the history of posthumanism without including Donna Haraway's "Cyborg Manifesto." Haraway, in a more politically aware mode, anticipates many of the posthuman aspects which Hayles puts forth twenty years later. She is also less bound by the hard sciences than Hayles seems to be.[4] Haraway attributes many qualities of a yet-named posthuman to the "cyborg";[5] specifically, Haraway's cyborg is a precursor to the "informed posthuman" which Hayles hopes we can become. Haraway's cyborg is—purposefully—hard to pin down. It shifts from an amorphous ontology to a localized, anthropomorphic being, and even to an ethereal presence. Conveniently for Haraway, not only *can* the cyborg be all of these things at once—it *must* be.

Haraway's cyborg is more politically motivated than Hayles' posthuman, however, and is presented as a bastardized, "blasphemous,"[6] technologically-mediated alternative to the liberal humanist subject. And, like Hayles' claim that we are already posthuman, Haraway contends that the cyborg is already among us. "The cyborg is our ontology; it gives us our politics. The cyborg is a condensed image of both imagination and material reality, the two joined centres structuring any possibility of historical transformation."[7] Haraway's portrayal of the cyborg as a blasphemous bastard-child is a clever technique which allows her to admit the necessity of the cyborg's liberal humanist "parenthood," thus making it possible for her to disavow that parenthood. As a blasphemer, the cyborg attempts to claim authority within a specific system of power and belief. The cyborg becomes an image that makes the rebellious posthuman—for lack of a better term—"cool."

The parenthood the cyborg repudiates is rooted in what Haraway believes is the deep-seated scientific and political traditions of the West, its traditions of "racist, male-dominated capitalism," progress, commodified culture, and—most importantly—"the tradition of reproduction of the self from the reflections of the other [reflections made possible by the Cartesian subject]." All of these are problematized and reconfigured by the cyborg ontology.[8]

Her cyborg stands as an offspring which refuses to go quietly, and is committed to stirring up discord in the Cartesian system from which it emerged (most notably the imposed distinctions between self and other), and gladly admits to its attempts to destabilize it. Ultimately, Haraway's "Cyborg Manifesto" is "an argument for *pleasure* in the confusion of boundaries and for *responsibility* of their construction."[9] Much of the "mission" of posthumanist discourse—its self-avowed goal to bring about a change in the way we view humanism and/or the human/technological relationship—has its roots in Haraway's manifesto.

Similar to Hayles' posthuman, Haraway's cyborg emphasizes a responsibility for creating and re-defining the boundaries which once marked the liberal humanist self; simply moving those boundaries outward to incorporate a larger, technified self would only serve to support "the awful apocalyptic *telos* of the 'West's' escalating dominations of abstract individuation, an ultimate self untied at last from all dependency."[10] The self/other dichotomy which the liberal humanist self depends upon is reconfigured.

The cyborg does not ascribe to the concept of an autonomous self, and admits its dependency on "the other" and the permeability of its own boundaries in order to survive. Interestingly enough, Haraway does not attempt to define or identify who (or what) "the other" might be. However, what we need to understand is that the cyborg—the precursor to the posthuman—accepts that it *cannot exist* without the other, or a "something else" in addition to itself.[11] The technologically mediated cyborg, in its more utopian incarnations, can imagine "a world without gender, which is perhaps a world without genesis, but maybe also a world without end."[12] The possibility for immortality is not as threatening in "Cyborg Manifesto" as it is in *How We Became Posthuman*, due to Haraway's admittedly utopian vision.[13]

Although Haraway does not seem to be as threatened by the possibility of immortality, the opportunities that technology presents within the context of a cyborg ontology can still lead us into the realm of Hayles' posthuman nightmare. The possibilities of technology (e.g., uploading our consciousness) can tempt us into replicating the qualities of the liberal humanist subject into the technological realm. If we look at a cyborg as a "ghost in the machine," where some essential, transcendent quality of self has been transferred, then we are guilty of reinscribing the humanist subject into a technological substrate. Similar to Hayles, this temptation comes from a reconceptualization of information which equates the self with an informational pattern.

Before Hayles was able to historicize the disembodiment of information, Haraway sensed the implications of its growing incorporeality: "Our best machines are made of sunshine; they are all light and clean because they are nothing but signals, electromagnetic waves, a section of a spectrum, and these machines are eminently portable, mobile. . . . People are nowhere near so fluid, being both material and opaque. Cyborgs are ether, quintessence."[14] Haraway moves almost too cleanly between the idea of an ethereal machine (note also how the "best machines" are ethereal), the very *not* ethereal human, and then back to the "cyborg" (which seems to embody both). Her concept of cyborg has shifts here, and becomes noticeably *less* anthropomorphic. Whether or not this was a conscious leap, it shows the difficulty in trying to characterize the human as a cyborg without radically altering the perception of the human itself. Also, the qualification of the "best" machines being ethereal de-emphasizes technology as artifact (which, conversely emphasizes the physicality of the human). This is a highly strategic maneuver, since an ethereal machine may be hard to grasp, but it is even harder for an ethereal machine to grasp us.

Haraway further emphasizes the importance of the body by identifying two contradicting perspectives by which the "cyborg world" can be viewed. The first resonates with Hayles' "posthuman nightmare," as a "final imposition of a grid of control" implied in the liberal humanist subject—appropriating the body (especially a woman's body) as something that can be easily equated with the ethereality of informatics and controlled and re-embodied through code and technology. This indicates the double-edged sword of the cyborg "quintessence" mentioned earlier. For Haraway, ethereality cannot be *imposed*. It is not something that a dominant power structure can "grant" or "bestow" upon an individual (especially a woman). Instead, it is something that can be "attained," again empowering and placing more emphasis on the human who would presumably—albeit by some unexplained means—attempt to achieve such ethereality.

The second perspective serves as the positive precursor to Hayles' "posthuman dream." Haraway states: "a cyborg world might be about lived social and bodily realities in which people are not afraid of their joint kinship with animals and machines, not afraid of permanently partial identities and contradictory standpoints."[15] Simply speaking, taking control of our own "informatic ethereality" is not to eschew our embodiedness. Instead, it is a way in which to recognize—and even celebrate—what amounts to an "interconnectedness" with the world. The path that Haraway traces here brings us closer to a fully "integrated" being for which the prospect of interfacing with technological systems and its compatibility with those systems is not an issue. But Haraway still maintains that some kind awareness of the boundaries would be inherent to the interface. Hayles later emphasizes this point by calling directly for a "refleshing" of the body. In Haraway, we see a less pressing need to re-claim the flesh that's being lost. The cyborg stands at more of a distance from humanity, offering itself as a middle-ground between present and future, rather than as an imposed ending to curtail humanity's obsolescence. The larger threat that Haraway perceives is not the loss of flesh, but its permeability to information.

Haraway and Code:
The True Cyborg Unwittingly Awakens

The re-crafting of our bodies—for better or for worse—would not be possible without a reconceptualization of information. Anticipating Hayles, Haraway considers information as a floating, "quantifiable element" which is able to flow freely across boundaries.[16] The specific qualities of those boundaries are themselves not important, because for Haraway, information serves to make *everything* permeable. Conversely, information *has the potential* to penetrate anything—or anyone. The latter has more ominous overtones.

Haraway sees the codification of human beings as a possible means by which the "sacredness" of the body is lost for the convenience of a seamless processing of signals in a "common language."[17] It is not difficult to understand how a "common language" of pure information would run counter to a feminist perspective, where the politics of homogenizing language would serve as a tool for silencing "other" voices. This possibility becomes the root of a nightmare scenario for Haraway, where the body itself is subject to a coded reconstruction:

> Furthermore, communications sciences and modern biologies are constructed by a common move—*the translation of the world into a problem of coding*, a search for a common language in which all resistance to instrumental control disappears and all heterogeneity can be submitted to disassembly, reassembly, investment, and exchange.[18]

Yet earlier, Haraway states that "The cyborg is a kind of disassembled and reassembled, postmodern collective and personal self. This is the self feminists must code."[19] It would seem that a "coded self" is a threat only when someone else has already coded it for you. The only way that this can be avoided is to understand (and perhaps appropriate) the "language of informatics" that has the potential to define us. Thus, in order to partake of the benefits of being a cyborg, we must be able to understand—perhaps even embrace—the means by which the self is coded. We must embrace the cyborg before the cyborg embraces us. We must, more than anything, *understand* our information.

We are reminded here of Hayles' view of what is "lethal" in the posthuman view, which was a "grafting of the posthuman onto a liberal humanist view of the self."[20] To graft implies an insertion. Insertion does not necessarily imply a violation, unless there is another person or force enacting the insertion. To embrace something—in this case, technology—is literally to enclose it, or envelop it. The difference here for Haraway is quite subtle, for it is possible for the two actions (insertion and embracing) to occur at once. Once again, we must turn to the idea of the informed posthuman in Hayles (and which is implied in Haraway's cyborg) versus the uninformed, reinscribed (and intentionally hyphenated) post-human. The post-human who seeks simply to reinscribe the self can never truly embrace technology, because he or she will always see technology as a separate entity. Inserting it, swallowing it, grafting it, wearing it, will always imply a self/other dichotomy. Uploading one's consciousness (considered to be the *self*) into a machine also reinscribes the subject in the belief that some *essence* of the self will still remain.

But once again, we see an unintended omission. Like Katherine Hayles does some twenty years later, Haraway also fails to take into account how an embrace in its own right can be considered a way in which the human can show dominance, taking control over the technological supplement so that it does not take control over—or erase—us. The self-other dichotomy of the liberal humanist subject is subverted only so much.

With this in mind, both Haraway and Hayles work under the assumption that there has to be *some* awareness of technology as an "other" which can be embraced. Haraway characterizes the relationship between human and technology as a much more intimate experience. For Haraway, the posthuman/cyborg embrace is represented as a *re-coded* (or perhaps more correctly, a *self-coded*) self, one that attempts to understand the nature of the constructed boundary between self and other (and therefore, human and machine), and accepts the necessity of the technological to realize the potential of our physical embodiment. For Haraway, this understanding is linked primarily to the ability to take charge of our coding—to be knowledgeable of the ways in which we are, literally, *informed* (shaped) by technology. This occurs through "writing," (what she later defines as "the power to signify") or, more specifically "Cyborg writing," which she describes as being "about the power to survive . . . on the basis of seizing the tools to mark the world that marked [women] as other."[21] Once again, the informed posthuman/cyborg requires technology to realize fully its potential.

Haraway's cyborg "dream" is, expectedly, more local and politicized than the dream Hayles advances in *How We Became Posthuman*. It challenges certain Western dualisms which contribute, in Haraway's view, to the "logics and practices of domination of women, people of colour, nature, workers, animals—in short, domination of all constituted as others."[22] It is only through "High tech culture" (read *technology*) that such dualisms can be challenged. These challenges serve only to blur the boundaries set by the liberal humanist subject, especially those between human and machine, and its relation to an embodied mind: "There is no fundamental, ontological separation in our formal knowledge of machine and organism, of technical and organic."[23] What is interesting here is how Haraway first locates the "connection" between machine and organism in the *ontological* realm, anticipating that placing technology *before* awareness itself would characterize the embrace as intrinsic to being human. Technology becomes a manner of achieving awareness, rather than simply a space in which the liberal humanist subject is reinscribed. The rhetorical maneuver she engages here hinges upon her use of the term *formal* knowledge. Haraway implies that a more intrinsic awareness that defies old Cartesian dualisms is possible, but that awareness still retains enough "self" to embrace technology. This missed opportunity is a lead which Hayles did not choose to follow, and which Haraway leaves tantalizingly open.

One of the consequences of becoming an informed cyborg is that "our sense of connection to our tools is heightened."[24] In this respect, Haraway admits that a physical coupling between human and machine does *not* have to be a violation. In fact, it can be a very real (and very beneficial) union. "For us, in imagination and in other practice, machines can be prosthetic devices, intimate components, friendly selves."[25] As she continues, the union of machine and human grows even closer, and becomes quite possibly a source of pleasure. Successful use and applications of technology become "an aspect of embodiment,"[26] rather than a furthering of the humanist agenda.

Haraway's discussion reaches its most insightful crescendo when she states:

> The machine is not an *it* to be animated, worshiped and dominated. The machine is us, our processes, an aspect of our embodiment. We can be responsible

for machines; *they* do not dominate or threaten us. We are responsible for boundaries; we are they.[27]

At first, the cyborg that Haraway proposes is not just a precursor to Hayles' posthuman; it is also a prescient (and very fleeting) metaphor for a fully—and technologically—evolved human being who paradoxically can no longer trace the boundary between itself and its technological "appendages." But tellingly, Haraway retreats as she maintains that we can claim responsibility for machines and that there are boundaries for which we are responsible (something which, as we will see in the following chapter, Oedipa Maas must deal with first-hand). Yet she leaves the image with an ambiguous "we are they."

As previously discussed, for the true cyborg, or posthuman, compatibility with information and the technological systems used to uncover that information would not be an issue, since the interface between self and the tools used to take in information would be utterly seamless. Haraway here implies (but does not follow up) something from which Hayles shies away, that the awareness of any kind of boundary between human and machine automatically precludes a true cyborg (or posthuman) experience. Indeed, the nature of her manifesto itself is designed to provoke more questions than it answers, but the implication this statement unearths raises the stakes of posthumanism from a possible epistemology to a possible *ontology*. But Haraway continues with her discussion, leaving this possibility as a tantalizing issue for others to consider.

All in all, by proposing the concept of the cyborg and consequently embracing the machine, Haraway reclaims the technological systems which might otherwise be used further to marginalize already-oppressed voices. In so doing, however, she has implied a *need* for technology both to overcome the already-present power structure inherent in the western subject, and to reach what amounts to the true potential of the re-coded, cyborg (posthuman) self. This need becomes more pronounced as Haraway claims that the cyborg is capable of re-envisioning fundamental epistemological boundaries. "There is a myth system waiting to become a political language to ground one way of looking at science and technology and challenging the informatics of domination—*in order to act potently*."[28]

One wonders if Haraway chose the word "potently" for irony's sake. However, the potency of the challenge she presents is still reliant on technology, and implies that without at least a technological "vocabulary" with which to engage the "informatics of domination," we stand marginalized and lacking efficacy.

> Taking responsibility for the social relations of science and technology . . . means embracing the skillful task of reconstructing the boundaries of daily life, in partial connection with others, in communication with all of our parts. It is not just that science and technology are possible means of great human satisfaction, as well as a matrix of complex dominations. Cyborg imagery can suggest a way out of the dualisms in which we have explained our bodies and our tools to ourselves.[29]

Technology becomes the means by which we achieve our potential as embodied, informed selves, and overcome what Haraway calls a "profound" injury that has somehow dismembered us. Unfortunately, she never truly identified what the cause of this "injury" was in the first place. The "regeneration" we require can only be achieved through becoming a knowledgeable cyborg.

As we will see in a later discussion of Lyotard's *Inhuman* and Scarry's *The Body in Pain*, the "injury" or trauma Haraway speaks of is one that has been inflicted by the very same bastardization of technology she invokes to rescue us from our "selves."

The Cyborg in Pain:
Relinquishing Consent in Order to Believe

Haraway's "Cyborg Manifesto" is an important first step backward into posthumanism's past, because it gives us insight into posthumanism's more ontological subtext. Hayles' "faith" in technology has been more or less neatly tucked away behind a grander vision of progress and understanding, but glimmers of awe—and even *hope*—become even more apparent once we gain more critical distance.

Both the posthuman and the cyborg literally embody a specific vision of technological power and possibility. Both hold in common an interesting paradox, that this technological other we are to become is also already *among us*. In both *How We Became Posthuman* and "Cyborg Manifesto," there is a rhetorical movement attempting to convince the reader that *we are* already the technological other. It is as if claiming one's cyborg or posthuman status is enough to bring it into being. But I believe that there is something more to these movements, something which resembles an attempt to evade a perceived threat. The technological models to which Hayles and Haraway hold us carry with them implications of *obsolescence*—the idea that the biological human alone is outmoded, unless it is supplemented with technology. Hayles and Haraway are implying that the human race, when held to technological standards, is already obsolete. Survival on both an individual and species-wide scale depends upon technology.

Technology has been a part of our collective experience since the first *homo sapiens* fashioned tools. But, as Scarry tells us, any technological artifact is a manifestation of a projected bodily attribute. That artifact "essentially takes over the work of the body, thereby freeing the embodied person of discomfort and thus enabling him to enter a larger realm of self-extension."[30] As those tools (and the systems of usage the arise around them) become more complex, more physical work is "outsourced" to the artifacts themselves.

Scarry uses the example of the decline of the Samurai in Japan to illustrate how "skill" is systematically pulled from human beings as technological systems become more advanced. The introduction of the gun and more complex systems of warfare made the Samurai class obsolete. A gun—in the hands of someone minimally trained to use it—could kill many more people in a shorter period of time than a highly-trained Samurai ever could. Human/technological development becomes marked by a *reduced* skill required to use technology. As humanity evolves, "more and more of the skill formerly required to use a weapon *is built into the new weapon itself,* thus increasingly freeing the participant from the amount of his life devoted to that act of participation.[31]

Although Scarry's example is a violent one, the basic model applies to almost all technological artifacts and systems. All we need to do is think about the difference between typing a document using a word-processor as opposed to typing one on a typewriter. While it takes skill to use both the word processor and the typewriter, even conservatively speaking, the word processor makes the process of revision and typesetting a much more simple act.

Taking the metaphor even further, Scarry points to nuclear weapons as the ultimate outsourcing of skill—to such an extent that *consent* itself is lost:

> So completely have the formerly embodied skills of weapon use been appropriated into the interior of the weapon itself that no human *skill* is now required; and because the need for human skills is eliminated, the human act of *consent* is eliminated. The *building in of skill* thus becomes in its most triumphant form, the *building out* of consent.[32]

Again, Scarry's example is a violent one, but even the most non-lethal and benevolent forms of technological systems represent a "building out" of skill. The argument can be made that to use these systems *effectively* requires a new kind of skill, but if we again look to the evolution of computers and their incorporation into the home, it becomes obvious that both skill *and* consent have been progressively taken out of human hands.[33] We may preside over more complex technological systems, but we become more distanced from the activities within them.

As technology advances, we increasingly value its self-maintaining aspects. The more independent the system becomes, the less necessary its human operator is. Of course, we can turn this model around and say that the independence of the system is a testimonial to *human* innovation. I would not disagree. But watching a system upgrade, update, and maintain itself generally brings with it a somewhat indirect satisfaction. We install anti-virus programs on our computers. It deletes a threat. We have no idea how it worked, but it did, and now we are happy—proud that we had the foresight to install the software in the first place, not that we single-handedly contained and deleted the virus ourselves. Indeed, even this example is dated: almost all computers sold today have anti-virus software pre-loaded at the point of purchase. So even *knowing* to install anti-virus software is itself "built out" of the average consumer.

While this is a necessarily small-scale example, it does not take much to apply this on the grand scale, especially in terms of posthumanism. The paradox of technology is that as it becomes more ubiquitous and advanced, we become more distanced from it conceptually. Sensing this, Hayles and Haraway call for us to "embrace" technological systems so that we can become more aware of them. Technology has reached the point where we now recognize our ability to distinguish it as a conceptual "other," which *seems* to move independently of human interaction. Although we know that all technology is the product of human innovation and creation, very few of the artifacts we—as individuals—use on a day-to-day basis are crafted directly and completely by us.[34]

What posthumanism seems to be reacting to is this distance, and the uneasy feeling that we are bestowing more independence to the technological other than we ought to be. It is an amorphous, but pervasive fear that plays itself out most directly in science fiction and literature, but increasingly seeps into our day to day lives. We can be happy that everything is working the way it should, but we do not understand how. The larger threat, however, is what happens when things *don't* work as they should, and we find ourselves not only without any capacity to make them right, but also in a state where we ourselves cannot work effectively. Human agency becomes inscribed in our technology, and if we cannot grasp that technology, or it has become unusable for whatever reason, it is our ability to act as humans that is affected.

So then, how does such a distance manifest itself? Here, we can borrow from Scarry's earlier model of analogical substantiation, where she maintains that the "felt characteristics of pain . . . can be appropriated away from the body and presented as something else."[35] Extrapolating from her own model of pain, Scarry applies the same dynamic to a more far-reaching, psychological dimension that occurs society-wide during a "crisis of belief":

> When some central idea or ideology or cultural construct has ceased to elicit a person's belief either because it is manifestly fictitious or because it has for some reason been divested of ordinary forms of substantiation—the sheer material factualness of the human body will be borrowed to lend that cultural construct the aura of "realness" and "certainty."[36]

I believe that the posthuman (and Haraway's Cyborg) represent a kind of analogical substantiation of the "central idea" or "cultural construct" of technology itself. It is a means to substantiate and anthropomorphize the technological other into something that can be embraced (and embrace back) in light of the "building out" of skill which characterizes technological development. The resulting "loss of consent" which occurs only serves to highlight the "incompleteness" of our bodies. To maintain our own physicality while using technological systems to "extend embodied awareness," we project our "humanness" into technological systems, borrowing the "material factualness" of our bodies.

Projecting humanness, however, is not a simple transference of our moods onto some artifact or system, nor is it just an anthropomorphizing of a system or object. As Scarry will show us, it is a "turning inside out" of the body in order to make ourselves compatible with systems which we feel have power over us.

The most simple object, according to Scarry, "is a lever across which a comparatively small change in the body at one end is amplified into a very large change in the object, animate or inanimate, at the other end."[37] The person who is using that tool feels empowered by the experience of making changes to his or her environment without running the risk of being directly affected by that change, or the failure of being unable to complete the task manually. For Scarry, the individual thus "objectifies his presence in the world through the alterability of his world" and what has been altered becomes a "record of his presence."[38] Use of technology is, in its most basic form, a means of "marking" the world, allowing the individual to "inhabit a space much larger than the small circle of his immediately present body."[39]

Scarry here articulates the "extended embodied awareness" which posthumanism so highly values. And if we follow the rhetoric of Hayles and Haraway closely, we will see that the idea of humans making their mark is a pervasive one—especially when both seem convinced that it is possible for technology to make *its own* mark on *us* if we're not careful. In fact, the more ominous the posthuman nightmare becomes, the more emphatically the imperative to hold onto the defining aspects of our humanity is conveyed. Hayles, sensing the largest threat, attempts to reclaim the body. Haraway, writing earlier and more distanced from more dehumanizing technologies, seeks to re-claim the tools which mark our presence.

Given Haraway's more politicized approach and concern that an "information society" has the potential to commodify and homogenize humans (especially women) by re-coding them, her emphasis of tools makes sense. Her concern with an alienation from the means to code becomes especially prescient, considering that, according to Scarry, the tool or technological artifact "is itself the concrete record of the connection between the worker and the object of his or her work; it is the path from the object back to its sentient source."[40] The tool (or artifact, or technological system) is both a means of affecting change in the world *and* a palpable record of one's connection with the world. "Across its concrete surface, the interior act and the exterior object become continuous."[41]

Perhaps Hayles' proclamation that we are already posthuman and Haraway's admission that the "machine is us" are attempts to re-claim a connection which they feel is either lost or in the process of becoming so. The tools themselves are manifestations of a larger technological other, and both Hayles and Haraway attempt to lay claim to that anologically substantiated concept of technological other. I believe that this loss is the "profound injury" which Haraway cryptically refers to toward the end of her manifesto.[42] Whether we were ever "connected" in the first place, the human being seems tragically incomplete and frail, and made more "solid" (meaning less permeable to information) in its physical embodiment. This would explain why the cyborg, in its ability to be both anthropomorphic *and* ethereal, stands as such a desirable alternative for Haraway.

Haraway's treatment of the cyborg as a shifting entity enables it to be simultaneously a) the technological "other" to which we aspire; b) the embodiment of the connection to that technological other; *and* c) a reconfigured version of human beings themselves. But what all of these different versions have in common is a very basic faith in the sustaining, transformative, and unifying power of technology. Furthermore—even when we are told that we *are* technology—technology itself is still treated as a distinct and powerful other.

Even in Haraway's most insightful moments, she seems to have great difficulty in uniting the human with the technological: "The machine is us," "We can be responsible for machines," "they do not dominate or threaten us," "we are they." At each turn, she attempts to lay claim to the technological while still rhetorically keeping it at the greatest distance possible: we/them, they/us, we/they. There is still a powerful subject/object dichotomy at work here that cannot be overcome through traditional means. For Haraway, the responsibility for machines is something which must be reclaimed. And, it would seem, our estrangement from these technological systems has given them great power.

But we cannot avoid the simple fact that we are, and always have been, responsible for both the creation *and* the maintaining of our technological systems. It is we who have empowered our machines to the extent that we believe them to be superior. The emerging pattern here is most similar to the structure of religious belief, where a superior deity is created in order to provide systems of control for a given society. Haraway's language—particularly her characterization of the cyborg as "blasphemous"—belies her "reverence" for technology and its overall *immunity* to the weaknesses of the human being. The cyborg is not susceptible to the same oppression that we—as humans—are vulnerable to.

The difficulty that arises is that Haraway (and even Hayles) portray humans as being vulnerable to technology. Their logic seems circular: we must use technology to save ourselves from technology. However, we must remember that technology only becomes lethal when it has been "grafted" onto the liberal humanist subject. Thus the gleaming, ethereal, clean technological cyborg remains innocent of the oppression of its human parents. In this model, "pure" technology is immune to human failings.

We, as humans, are "wounded" because we are woundable; technology, god-like, is not. Turning to Scarry now, we see the similarity between god and technology most clearly:

> The invented god and its human inventor . . . are differentiated by the immunity of the one and the woundablility of the other; and if the creature is not merely *woundable* but already and permanently *wounded*, handicapped, or physically marred in some way . . . then that individual is asserted to exist at an even greater moral distances from God than does the "normal" person.[43]

Technology is effectively given power over us as the human/technological relationship is inverted. It has the ability to wound us, and the moments when it does not make it seem all the more benign. This is how technology gains the power to "save" us. If it destroys us, it does so because we "deserved it" because of our hubris and our inability to respect its power. When it saves us, it does so because of our *faith* in its power.

As humans, we are ultimately woundable because of our bodies. Technology, on the other hand, is immune because it has no body (recall Haraway's claim that our "best machines" are ethereal and clean). By presenting our "best" technological systems as ethereal, Haraway has conceptually distanced the human from technology, making the possibility of any kind of effective tangible interface close to impossible. If we want to get closer to—and interact with—our best technology, we are forced to use more intangible methods. This relationship pushes interface out of the physical and into the realm of the metaphysical. Belief, according to Scarry, is characterized by an "intensification of the body and projections of its attributes outward onto a disembodied object."[44] In this light, Hayles' call for a "refleshing" of the body is transformed into a call to strengthen our faith.

Also, the refleshing Hayles calls for is not a refleshing at all. Instead of highlighting the specific strengths of the body, her concept of refleshing is actually a reconceptualization of the body, making it more *metaphysically* compatible with technological systems. By this logic, if we are unable to enhance our physical and mental capabilities, we are expressing doubt. To doubt the validity of our bodies *in light of our faith in machines* becomes "a failure to remake one's own interior in the image of God, to allow God to enter and alter one's self."[45] This "surrendering of our interior," in Scarry's words, "*is itself belief*— the endowing of the most concrete and intimate parts of oneself with an objectified referent, the willing re-reading of events within the realm of sentience as themselves attributes of the realm of self-extension and artifice."[46] While it may seem a stretch to substitute "God" for "technology" or "machine" here, the structure of belief is the same. In many ways, technology is viewed with the same reverence, and the same power as a deity.

Most importantly, however, what this model eventually accomplishes is an explanation of how technology has been effectively transformed from an object of human making to a god-like other which has the power to save us and kill us at the same time. Our belief in technology is, following Scarry's model, an object that has been created and "credited with more reality (and all that is entailed in greater 'realness,' more power, more authority) than oneself."[47]

The effects of this complex dynamic are far-reaching. Our feelings of inadequacy are emphasized. We search for a means of interface that never seems "good enough." And even when we do find a computer, cell phone, or even automobile that works well for our present needs, we are always aware that inevitably there is something better that is just beyond our grasp. Information as a concept is further abstracted; we seek out better ways to store, organize, and uncover it, but we do so without the means to understand it.

Yet, the posthuman expectation is that we take responsibility for our information and our relationship to the systems we use—paradoxically through the very systems for which we are asked to take responsibility. My own argument suggests that our human frailty is brought to the forefront as we find ourselves without the proper "apparatus" to understand the systems which we believe define us. But, as will become apparent, without any apparatus, humans fall to one distinctly human attribute to mediate the world: narrative. Aptly, it is through narrative that our "posthuman condition" will be most effectively illustrated.

Notes

1. Scarry, *Body in Pain*, 207.
2. Hayles, *Posthuman*, 5.
3. Hayles, *Posthuman*, 5.
4. Possibly due to the fact that Hayles began her career as a chemist.
5. Haraway's use of the term cyborg diverges from its original scientific usage as a cybernetic organism, especially since she moves away from the idea of "control system" that the term cybernetics usually delineates. While one can substitute "posthuman" for cyborg in general terms, Haraway's usage implies a more anthropomorphic, cohesive entity. It is more or less of an embodied precursor to the posthuman, but less scientifically bound than Hayles' term. For the most part, Haraway's "cyborg" is a useful metaphor on which for her to fall back, making it more organic and easier to characterize as a personality that works against the latent oppression present in the liberal humanist subject Haraway calls us to resist.
6. "Blasphemous" is an apt choice of words here, since blasphemy implies a recognition of the power of some kind of sacred entity, and is an attempt to claim that power or the attributes of that entity for oneself. It is a convenient metaphor for attempting to claim power "within the system"; or attempting to use the system against itself.
7. Donna Haraway, "A Cyborg Manifesto: Science, Technology, and Socialist-Feminism in the Late Twentieth Century," in *Simians, Cyborgs, and Women: The Reinvention of Nature* (New York: Routledge, 1991), 150. This is an interesting and recurrent image in posthumanism (the idea that the we are already posthuman or that the posthuman/cyborg is "already among us"), as if to invoke the posthuman is to make it happen or bring it closer to being. It also implies an almost obsessive desire for the posthuman to make itself known in the present, rather than as something which will inevitably happen in the future.
8. Haraway, "Cyborg Manifesto," 150.
9. Haraway, "Cyborg Manifesto," 150.
10. Haraway, "Cyborg Manifesto," 150-51.
11. It is tempting to identify the "other" here as technology itself. In this respect, the other operates in the same fashion that the "post" does for the posthuman—as an addition, a component that is not human, but that must be supplemented in order for us to achieve full humanity.
12. Haraway, "Cyborg Manifesto," 150.
13.This might be due, in part, to the fact that Haraway's work precedes Hayles' by about two decades, when technological systems such as e-mail and the internet were not as ubiquitous as they are today. The characterization of the cyborg as "already among us"

rather than the declaration that "we are already posthuman" reflects less pressure to present a "conclusion" to the human.

14. Haraway, "Cyborg Manifesto," 153.

15. Haraway, "Cyborg Manifesto," 154.

16. Haraway, "Cyborg Manifesto," 164.

17. Haraway, "Cyborg Manifesto," 163.

18. Haraway, "Cyborg Manifesto," 164.

19. Haraway, "Cyborg Manifesto," 163. Haraway addresses feminists here out of concern that women in an increasingly technological society stand to be "techno-digested." "The dichotomies between mind and body, animal and human, organism and machine, public and private, nature and culture, men and women, primitive and civilized are all in question ideologically. The actual situation of women is their integration/exploitation into a world system of production/reproduction and communication called the informatics of domination. . . . One important route for reconstructing socialist-feminist politics is through theory and practice addressed to the social relations of science and technology." (163)

20. Hayles, *Posthuman*, 286.

21. Haraway, "Cyborg Manifesto," 175. The fact that Haraway privileges writing here speaks directly to Hansen's contention in *Embodying Technesis* that discourse about technology so often privileges the *logos*, rather than directly examine the technological *as technology*.

22. Haraway, "Cyborg Manifesto," 177.

23. Haraway, "Cyborg Manifesto," 178.

24. Haraway, "Cyborg Manifesto," 178.

25. Haraway, "Cyborg Manifesto," 178.

26. Haraway, "Cyborg Manifesto," 180.

27. Haraway, "Cyborg Manifesto," 180.

28. Haraway, "Cyborg Manifesto," 181 (emphasis mine).

29. Haraway, "Cyborg Manifesto," 181.

30. Scarry, *Body in Pain*, 144.

31. Scarry, *Body in Pain*, 151-52. (emphasis mine). Once again, we see this theme commonly revisited in various science fiction franchises. In the classic *Star Trek* episode, "The Ultimate Computer," the M-5 computer is put in charge of the *Enterprise* for war games exercises, ending with tragic consequences. In "For the World is Hollow and I have Touched the Sky," a humanoid race, adrift on an asteroid-sized starship, the *Yona-da,* is so "cared for" by the central computer that they aren't even aware that they are on a starship traveling through space. In the newest iteration of *Battlestar Galactica*, the "Cy-lons"—a race of robots created by humans—battle for sovereignty and even create a subspecies of themselves. Of course, the *Matrix* and *Terminator* films also engage the theme of developing technology beyond the scope of human control.

32. Scarry, *Body in Pain*, 152.

33. The skill aspect is somewhat obvious: To even have access to a computer in the late 1940s required highly specialized training. The computing power of a machine which once needed an entire support staff to operate can now be found in the smallest of PDAs (personal digital assistants) and home computers. To address consent: As I write this sentence, my computer has just "updated itself" automatically—downloading the necessary software to keep itself running effectively. While I initially gave my "consent" for these processes to occur when I set up the application, I did so once. Most of the time, I have no idea when these updates occur. We can also see the outsourcing of skill occur in

the development of more comprehensive safety systems in cars. Anti-lock brakes and vehicle stability controls help the driver maintain control of the vehicle, but require a certain "un-learning" of the skill of pumping one's brakes and steering into a skid. More advanced safety systems now will apply the brakes for the driver if the driver gets too close to the car in front of them. On the horizon are safety systems which "interpret" the pattern of traffic and/or obstacles ahead of the vehicle and will apply the brakes before the driver is even aware of a hazard; if a deer were to jump in the road or a child were to dart out in front of the car, the car would avoid the accident before the driver's reflexes could engage. In this manner, it could be said that the car (or more accurately, the computer that controls the car) "knows" that something will occur before the driver does.

34. Even for those who "build" their own computers, the are in reality only assembling them. The chips, casings, wiring, fans, etc. are ready-made. Very few—if any—have the capacity, skill, or resources to create each individual component from scratch.

35. Scarry, *Body in Pain*, 14.

36. Scarry, *Body in Pain*, 14.

37. Scarry, *Body in Pain*, 175.

38. Scarry, *Body in Pain*, 175.

39. Scarry, *Body in Pain*, 175.

40. Scarry, *Body in Pain*, 176.

41. Scarry, *Body in Pain*, 176

42. "We have all been injured, profoundly. We require regeneration, not rebirth, and the possibilities for our reconstitution include the utopian dream of the hope for a monstrous world without gender" Scarry, *Body in Pain*, 181. Interestingly enough, she begins this section with the image of the severed limb of a salamander. Haraway seems to be sensing not simply a distancing of humans from technological systems, but a complete severing.

43. Scarry, *Body in Pain*, 183.

44. Scarry, *Body in Pain*, 197.

45. Scarry, *Body in Pain*, 197.

46. Scarry, *Body in Pain*, 205.

47. Scarry, *Body in Pain*, 205.

Chapter Two

The Crying of Lot 49
and
Posthuman Subjectivity:
Conditional Humanity

One of the problems with achieving posthuman subjectivity as presented by Hayles and Haraway is that both make the assumption that the connection between human and technological other has already been made. In *How We Became Posthuman* and "Cyborg Manifesto," posthumanism is presented as a mode of inquiry to be enacted *after* an interface has already been established, without taking into account the process by which humans—believing technology to be a superior other—try (often unsuccessfully) to enact. The texts put forth a posthumanism which characterizes human agency as conditional to our compatibility with information, and the technological artifacts and systems we use to process that information. They imply that our effective use of technology is thus directly proportional to the quality of the interface between ourselves and the technological system which we use. Achieving any goal requires a technological apparatus of some sort. If we cannot use that apparatus effectively, we are thwarted from achieving that goal.

For the posthuman, human efficacy (what Hayles would define as a fully embodied awareness) is only as good as the apparatus through which we achieve that efficacy. Thus, before we can complete a task, we must find the proper apparatus to complete it. The difficulty we are faced with is that the task itself has the potential to be eclipsed by the search for the right object (artifact, technological system, etc.) which will help us complete that task. On a larger scale, the systems through which we are directed to achieve a posthuman subjectivity run the risk of distracting us from that very goal. The objective is eclipsed by the object. What technological object, system, or combination of them will allow us to see what we need to see; to do what we need to do; or to be what we need to be? Early posthumanist discourse focuses its attention on what happens *after* that apparatus has been found, without addressing the implications involved in having to find the right apparatus in the first place.

Thomas Pynchon's *The Crying of Lot 49* illustrates this key gap in early posthumanist discourse by presenting a character who remains in a constant state of reserve until she can find the right apparatus to begin her "quest." The story of Oedipa Maas is literally the story of the human in early posthuman discourse—the human who is aware that the opportunity for an expanded "embodied awareness" exists, but cannot find the right means to achieve it.

From the start, Oedipa feels inadequate and ill-prepared to achieve her singular task: "to execute the will" of her deceased ex-lover, Pierce Inverarity. Oedipa's quest is symbolic of the human attempt to mediate the boundaries between itself and what is perceived as superior systems, and explicates the process and difficulties of "taking responsibility" for those boundaries. Oedipa feels that her defining system, the Tristero,[1] has the power to sustain, destroy, and, most importantly, acknowledge her existence and her pain in terms which she can understand and recognize. She believes, abstractly, that this acknowledgement will give her power. Oedipa attempts to embrace the Tristero, but she does not have a satisfactory means of doing so.

For Oedipa Maas, her journey is framed by her need to make sense of the multiple technological and narrative systems she believes are in play, and ultimately to take responsibility for the world she is projecting. She feels herself to be implicated in a larger plot, the boundaries of which are intrinsically linked to the ever-expanding Inverarity estate. Dogged by feelings of inadequacy, Oedipa's attempts to, in her own words, "sort everything out" are repeatedly thwarted by eerie coincidences, complex patterns of events, and legal complexities.

Aside from her feelings of inadequacy, the only real consistency of Oedipa's narrative is her recognition of a ubiquitous electronic "buzzing" that intermittently comes in and out of her "range of perception." Even though she can't hear it all the time, she can feel it, and relies on its presence as evidence of a higher system at work, "keeping it all together." Manifestations of technology surround Oedipa: she repeatedly finds herself "stared at" by the "dead eye" of television tubes; most of the major plot development occurs near or in relations to the Yoyodyne aerospace plant; and she often characterizes San Narciso (Inverarity's home town) as a circuit board. *The Crying of Lot 49* anticipates the rise of the posthuman by characterizing Oedipa as primed to privilege technological systems—things she does not understand—as a kind of other which is superior to her. It also calls attention to the ongoing silence in posthumanism regarding the failure of interface that so often plagues us in our attempts to achieve a "true" posthuman subjectivity, or what Hayles would call fully "embodied awareness."

Middle Spaces:
Between Posthuman Farsightedness
and Postmodern Nearsightedness

She had looked down at her feet and known, then, because of a painting, that what she stood on had only been woven together a couple of thousand of miles away in her own tower, was only by accident known as Mexico, and so Pierce had taken her away from nothing, there'd been no escape. What did she so desire escape from? Such a captive maiden, having plenty of time to think, soon realizes that her tower, its height and architecture, are like her ego only incidental: that what really keeps her where she is is magic, anonymous and malignant, visited on her from outside and for no reason at all.[2]

Literary criticism regarding *The Crying of Lot 49* primarily focuses on Oedipa's attempts to make sense of a random and chaotic world. From a postmodern standpoint, Oedipa's attempt to find meaning *is* her quest, and it stands in direct opposition to entropy—a force which threatens her with dissolution. As a self-reflexive text, *Lot 49* also chronicles the process of reading itself: Oedipa stands in for the reader, who is also trying to make sense of the text. David Seed echoes the consensus of critics when he points out that Oedipa's journey mirrors the readers' attempts to make sense out of the novel itself.[3] In a postmodern world, questioning the appearances of things is often a prerequisite to navigating through a deconstructed reality. *The Crying of Lot 49* becomes the story of a woman attempting to assign significance to the signs around her. Patrick O'Donnell notes that the novel itself takes the form of a question, representing our desire for meaning, and our continuing attempts to read significance into the world.[4]

While I do not disagree that Oedipa is trying to make sense of her world, to address difficulties inherent in posthuman subjectivity, we need to take the story one step further by taking one step back. Although Oedipa's stated goal is to "sort everything out," what Oedipa is *actually* looking for is a means to engage the system so that she *can* sort it all out. Indeed, to make sense of the world is the avowed purpose of Oedipa's quest; but to look at the novel in a more posthuman light is to accept this desire for understanding as an integral part of Oedipa's attempt to be as fully human and *effective* as possible. To look at the posthuman aspect of the novel is to concentrate on Oedipa's quest for an apparatus through which she may gain such understanding. Ultimately, we see that Oedipa's quest for the right apparatus is an impossible one. What Oedipa wants is what the posthuman wants: a seamless, non-threatening interface with a technological superior other, via an acknowledgement of the human subject. Oedipa wants to recognize herself in the Tristero—literally—in her own terms, much like Haraway's cyborg subjectivity puts the human in control of the means by which they are inscribed in a technological lifeworld.

By doing so, we can pull Oedipa out of the postmodern paradigm she's been imprisoned in—a paradigm which actually de-emphasizes Oedipa's efficacy by glorifying her submission to the system as a form of postmodern heroism, where her self-inflicted marginalization represents an attempt to gain a needed perspective. There is no doubt that Oedipa is indeed a reader of signs and text,[5] or that she exists in some kind of middle space, "between a reductive literalism in which words are mere tools standing for things, and a speculative symbolism in which words are signs capable of pointing toward realities which transcend those signs."[6] As an "executrix," Oedipa is trying to be a reader. The middle space she occupies resembles a posthuman equivalent—a space after humanism and before the transcendent, technified subjectivity of the fully embodied awareness which posthumanism promises.

Being in such a position of responsibility would automatically make Oedipa very weary of acting rashly and misinterpreting the signs she is being shown. And at the rate at which those signs are being uncovered, Oedipa is, as Eddins explains, running the risk of being saturated to the extent that the Tristero will destroy her sense of humanity.[7] But characterizing Oedipa's hesitation as a "heroic waiting" as Alan Wilde does[8] is to miss the reason why Oedipa feels trapped in the first place. The entropy around her increases, and Oedipa cannot mediate the vast amount of information to which she's exposed. She cannot effectively make sense of anything until she finds the proper apparatus with which to do so.

While a direct comparison of postmodernism and posthumanism would be outside the scope of this text, it would not be incorrect to say that posthumanism itself is a search for the right tool by which the postmodern condition can be engaged. Eddins succinctly puts the postmodern approach to *Lot 49* in perspective when he states that the "point" of the novel is "put in the form of a question: it is conceivably a quest without end, an inquiry into and dramatization of our incessant desire for meaning, our will to generate signs and significance wherever we plant our feet. Framing this desire *as* a question is one of the hallmarks of postmodern literature."[9] What makes the text posthuman, however, is that our protagonist feels that she does not possess the means to articulate the right question, and is in search of the proper apparatus to "frame the desire" itself. Until Oedipa can find the tools she needs go engage her system, she is held in reserve.

What will give us the most insight into posthumanism, however, is focusing on what Oedipa *expects* to gain from the system. Through *The Crying of Lot 49*, we will see that what the posthuman is still looking for is a perfect reflection of itself in technology—a perfectly technified other that can "suffer with" it and perfectly articulate the pain of the human condition.

Without Apparatus: Making Sense of the World Through Posthuman Assumptions

> Having no apparatus except gut fear and female cunning to accept this formless magic, to understand how it works, how to measure its field strength, count its lines of force, she may fall back on superstition, or take up a useful hobby like embroidery, or go mad, or marry a disk jockey. If the tower is everywhere and the knight of deliverance no proof against its magic, what else?[10]

Through examining Oedipa's attempts at mediating her world, *The Crying of Lot 49* provides us with examples and insights into all of the central criteria of posthumanism. Oedipa, occupying a marginalized space, is seeking answers without knowing the right questions. But the one consistency in her attempts is the technological frame through which she tries to articulate those questions. In this manner, Oedipa's quest falls in line with early posthumanism's core assumptions. First and foremost, information (without form, but endowed with power) has a privileged status in the novel, so much so that Oedipa herself deems "sorting everything out" to be the overriding condition which delays her from executing Inverarity's will. She perpetually uncovers all manner of connections and significant data, but feels that she cannot glean any meaning from it without some kind of help.

Very quickly, as Oedipa feels the pangs of a posthuman inadequacy, the process of sorting information (rather than understanding it) eclipses all else. Understanding "how it works" depends upon "measuring field strength" and counting "lines of force"—all representation of data that can only be mediated through technological means. Even the term "execute" itself has the technological connotation of running a program. Not only is Oedipa framed by technological metaphors, she also uses them in an attempt to understand and stake a claim in what is becoming an expanding world; a world threatening her with insignificance.

Her feelings of inadequacy lead us to the next posthuman criteria—viewing the body as a prosthesis. Although Oedipa does not wish to forgo her body, she is often limited by it—both literally and figuratively. She has no idea what field strength or lines of force are, let alone how to *use* that information effectively. She cannot understand the more technical aspects of her quest. She finds herself physically, mentally, and emotionally weak and ill-prepared for the task at hand. Her body seems both cumbersome and incomplete at the same time. While she may not want to abandon her body all together, her physicality often gets in the way. What she is looking for is a posthuman subjectivity, one that will allow (and empower) her to achieve her task, complete it, through understanding her role in the system itself. In other words, to be "aware" of the boundaries.

The most graphic example of this comes when the lawyer, Metzger, who is initially supposed to assist Oedipa in executing the will, instead objectifies her as a potential conquest (threatening her boundaries). Here, Metzger is an agent of the system (the Tristero). Thus, his attempts to bed her are symbolic of the posthuman nightmare scenario of being embraced by the system—grafting itself onto (and into) her. Initially, Oedipa tries to fend him off through literally *adding* layers to herself—most apparent when they participate in a game of "Strip Botticelli." During the game, Oedipa excuses herself to the bathroom, and then puts on every piece of clothing she owns. This acts as a means to protect herself and gain control over the game, and over Metzger, who, as an agent of the system, is the only person who seems to understand the legal machinations she must engage. Metzger becomes a tool which Oedipa finds she cannot properly use, and he ultimately uses her when he "wins" the game.

Oedipa eventually lumbers out of the bathroom, covered in layers of clothing. Even though she can barely move—making her less effective—it becomes her way of dealing with an ongoing "stripping" that occurs as she progresses through the novel. She feels *more embodied* as the system continually thwarts her. Consequently, she is never able to find a true reflection of herself—due specifically to repeated, direct *technological* interference. At one point, an errant aerosol can shatters every reflective surface in the room:

> The can knew where it was going, she sensed, or something fast enough, God or a digital machine, might have computed in advance the complex web of its travel; but she wasn't fast enough, and knew only that it might hit them at any moment, at whatever clip it was doing, a hundred miles an hour [the can breaks all reflective surfaces in the room]. . . . She could imagine no end to it.[11]

Oedipa was "not fast enough" to figure out where the can was headed (to stave off further destruction of the means by which she sees herself), but "God or a digital machine" was. Already, Oedipa—in posthuman terms—privileges technological systems at her own expense. An object as small (and unintelligent) as a spray-can seems to be smarter than she is, since it is fully integrated into the system (as Metzger was). Technology here doesn't necessarily block her attempts to interact with it; instead, it seems to stop her from knowing *herself.* Or it at least stops her from achieving a perfectly reflected self integrated into the system.

Instead, Oedipa sees only caricatures of herself, specifically in the parking lot of the aptly named "Echo courts" in the city of San Narciso, where a large animatronic nymph welcomes the guests. The nymph's face was "much like Oedipa's," and greeted her when she "pulled into the lot."[12] She sees representations of herself, knows that they are significant, but cannot yet articulate why or how they are. It is as if Oedipa is being lifted out of her "self," and being presented with different, technified bodies—none of which she feels are her own.

Oedipa's situation articulates a literary manifestation of the dream and nightmare scenarios of posthumanism. Linked with her desire to find the proper apparatus is an implied desire to see herself reflected in the Tristero—but reflected in the way *she* wants to be reflected. Oedipa wants to see herself *as she thinks she is*, and not as what she believes is a distorted representation. To see oneself accurately reflected in the system is part of the posthuman dream. To see ourselves would show us that the system *understood* who we are, and has no designs to erase us, making the system safer to engage and ultimately safe to embrace.

The fact that Oedipa never can gain an accurate reflection of herself, (in a sense being re-written, or re-coded by the Tristero) points to the nightmare counterpart of the posthuman dream. While Oedipa is not—as such nightmare scenarios often depict—grafting technological artifacts onto and into her own body (Metzger notwithstanding), these representations of her within the system characterize an unwilling embrace. The system is showing her its own "version" of her, one which she recognizes, but had no part in inscribing in the first place. In essence, the system did not have permission to represent her. She had already been inscribed within it before she had the chance to effectively engage it (embrace it) herself. The situation further de-emphasizes the effectiveness of Oedipa's physicality, making the possibility of a complete dissolution even more threatening.

This leads to the third aspect of posthumanism—viewing consciousness itself as an epiphenomenon, a prospect that becomes most apparent (and threatening) to her when she meets with Randolph Driblette, author of the play "The Courier's Tragedy" (a play which eerily reflects Oedipa's own quest, and also mentions the term "Tristero" for the first time). Oedipa is most taken by his contention that he himself is "responsible" for the world he inhabits, and that if he were to disappear, his projections of everything, including her, would disappear with him.

> "If I were to dissolve in here," speculated the voice out of the drifting steam, "be washed down the drain into the Pacific, what you saw tonight would vanish too. You, that part of you so concerned, God knows how, with that little world, would also vanish."[13]

Of course, such a possibility plays upon Oedipa's growing unease at the state of her "world," making her more sensitive to issues of existence itself. Oedipa's human subjectivity is characterized as being incidental to the overall narrative which is unfolding before her, reflecting a posthuman fear that technologically mediated subjectivity can render consciousness as incidental in human evolution. The reaction of posthumanism is to take back control, or the means of expressing consciousness itself.

In *The Crying of Lot 49*, the added dimension of responsibility suddenly brings Oedipa closer to coming to terms with her role as executrix of Inverarity's will, but it also deepens her fear by implicating that she has more responsibility than she once thought—that she could, in fact, be projecting her world. Scarry addresses this best when she states that "the recognition that one has been unselfconsciously dwelling in the midst of one's own creation by witnessing this derealization of the made thing is a terrifying and self-repudiating process."[14] Oedipa faces that prospect with an already tenuous sense of self. So, on one level, being a "projector" could conceivably help to combat Oedipa's increasing sense of disintegration by giving her a tenable point of view, and thus placing her in a position of control. It is also an attractive metaphor, because a projector does not have to project itself in order to be effective. However, the question remains, would Oedipa know how to be a projector?

When Driblette commits suicide and Oedipa does not cease to exist, she realizes that she must rely on her own half-hearted, and uninformed, acts of projection:

> It was part of her duty, wasn't it, to bestow life on what had persisted, to try to be what Driblette was, the dark machine in the center of the planetarium, to bring the estate into pulsing stelliferous meaning, all in a soaring dome around her.[15]

It is this added codicil to what Oedipa *believes* is expected of her that serves to complicate her overall quest. Not only is she to bring the estate into meaning, but into "pulsing" and "stelliferous"[16] meaning; alluding to a living, almost transcendent meaning which she is simply not equipped to enact, deliver, or even understand. How to procedurally "bestow life" upon anything is beyond her.

Furthermore, Oedipa is aspiring to be more machine-like. She equates herself with a projector, thus holding herself up to a technological standard which she has no hope of actually achieving. In keeping with the projector metaphor, Oedipa feels that being able to project her world would be akin to understanding it. If she had all the information that she needed, she would project the Tristero clearly and thus understand its extent as well as her own role in it.

Turning to posthumanism, Oedipa's desire to *be* (exist) as efficiently and effectively as a technological artifact speaks to the posthuman desire to make consciousness more compatible with machines. This compatibility would allow the biological human to achieve a more direct relationship with information itself. Her situation brings to the forefront an issue which posthumanism sets up, but does not fully address.

In order to become more compatible with technological systems in general, we must aspire to some aspects of technology; we must admit that on some level, technology possesses some quality which is superior to us. Furthermore, by these standards, to be *more* human we paradoxically need to be *more* like our technology. The disparity between our human abilities and the added abilities the supplement of technology would grant us creates a *need*. The less empowered we feel, the more we need technology.

Posthumanism places achieving our full humanity (or fully embodied awareness) as conditional to our ability to understand our own information (the data the defines us)—information that can only be uncovered through the right technological system. By setting up the right means of interface as a condition to achieving "full" humanity, it shifts our goal, so to speak. Instead of focusing on how our information/technology can benefit us as humans, we instead run the risk of becoming obsessed with finding the perfect means of interface. By not addressing the "need" that the conditional status of humanity creates, posthumanism ignores the most human aspect of our increasingly technologically mediated experience. It also fails to address the expression of that need as it is manifested in our search for the right interface to mediate information. Posthumanism places itself *after* the interface has been made. In doing so, posthumanism becomes blind to the fact that it is actually looking for a technological other which fully recognizes the human as human, and can thus perfectly articulate our human suffering for us.

The Crying of Lot 49 points out what happens *before* this fully realized posthuman state is actually reached, and eventually brings into question whether or not that state can actually be reached while still holding onto some aspect of human subjectivity. Can we say that Oedipa *is* posthuman, simply because she attempts to make sense of her world through technological metaphors? If we read Hayles one way, then yes, Oedipa does meet the criteria of having a "posthuman point of view."[17] And we cannot forget that Hayles herself states that those criteria are "assumptions" meant to be "suggestive rather than prescriptive."[18] But having a posthuman point of view does not make one "truly" posthuman—if we follow the arguments set out by Hayles herself regarding her dream scenarios of posthumanism where one reaches a "fully embodied awareness" via technological systems.

By not addressing how our need for technology manifests itself, and situating itself after the connection has already been made, posthumanism falls victim to a constant, halting quality—advancing and retreating: We *are already* posthuman, but really we're not; we have a posthuman point of view, but not a true posthuman subjectivity. The same holds true for Haraway's cyborg: it is already among us, but we've not achieved it yet, even though the cyborg is *us*. Posthumanism, in this light, seems to be more of a "middle state," or suspended present moment that comes between humanism and posthumanism.[19] Hayles herself, soon *after* outlining the criteria of a posthuman point of view, admits:

> I view the present moment as a critical juncture when interventions might be made to keep disembodiment from being rewritten, once again, into prevailing concepts of subjectivity. I see the deconstruction of the liberal humanist subject as an opportunity to put back into the picture the flesh that continues to be erased in contemporary discussions about cybernetic subjects.[20]

The agenda here is a noble one, and echoes Donna Haraway's desire to "reclaim the tools of inscription" that encode the body and render it not only more compatible with information, but also make it more susceptible to losing agency in an increasingly technified world. The "present moment" which Hayles describes and Haraway implies is vast, but there is a hint of desperation in these proclamations: a belief that to declare oneself a cyborg or a posthuman is enough to at least stave off some kind of appropriation into a technified, datafied future. It becomes a means of "concluding" humanism without "completing" it.

The problem here, and one which will become most apparent in following chapters, is that if we take away the "specialness" of the present moment (i.e., "we stand at a critical juncture"), we—as human beings—have *always* been defined by the technological systems (no matter how primitive) we use. That is not to negate posthumanism as an important mode of discourse; in fact, I believe that posthumanism itself is important in helping us understand the present technological *idiom* through which we currently negotiate the world, since the "posthuman" point of view that Hayles outlines—especially in terms of our relationship to information—*is* and has been at work actively shaping our human subjectivity since at least the Second World War.[21] But posthumanism has planted its flag in the wrong spot.

What we are left with, then, is a post-human subjectivity that is informed by a technological idiom in which information, and consequently experience itself, is dependent upon some kind of apparatus through which it can be mediated. That apparatus *does not* have to be a solid technological artifact or a topological technological system; it can also be metaphorical in nature. However, those metaphors are *technological*. Thus, when Oedipa is first "charged" with the task of executing Pierce's will, not only is she presented to us by Pynchon in technological terms, Oedipa as a character enframes her world through technological metaphors.

From a postmodern perspective, Oedipa is attempting to make meaning. From a posthuman perspective, however, Oedipa is attempting to *find the means to make meaning*. *The Crying of Lot 49* and its posthuman ·leanings raise the issue that perhaps the postmodern condition has become so widespread and deeply rooted—the world has been so subjected to deconstruction and fragmentation—that meaning itself has become irrelevant. Concurrently, reaching full human potential (in posthuman terms, fully embodied awareness) is impossible until we find the right means to achieve it. The point is no longer to find answers, it is to find the best way to find answers. Like Oedipa, we find ourselves in a continuing state of reserve, hoping for a better interface to come along to make our relationship with information easier.

Posthuman Suffering and the Nefastis Machine

It is important to keep in mind that this kind of postponement of efficacy that posthumanism implies does not necessarily attach itself to every technological metpahor, artifact, and/or system of use. In this regard, technology is like language, in that it only announces itself as technology when it fails. We are all surrounded with technological systems and artifacts, and when they operate smoothly and allow us to complete the task at hand, they conceptually remain at a comfortable and necessary distance.

We are not aware of the pencil as a tool until the point breaks, and it no longer functions as it is supposed to. We get a little closer to the real-world implications of posthuman suffering if we think back to the moments when we only had one pencil at hand—and no sharpener around. A mere annoyance, unless, of course, the thought in my head *had* to be written down just then—or if I had just witnessed an accident from my window, and needed to jot down the license plate number of the car speeding away. In such a scenario, not only am I not able to record the number, but—having a terrible mind for memorization—I *know* I will not remember it.

In multiple registers, I am frustrated: how could I have only *one* pencil? How could I have no sharpener? Why do I lack the ability/discipline to memorize the number? With no sharpener, I look for a knife; it won't be the perfect tool to sharpen the pencil, but it will do. Inevitably, there is no knife close enough to be useful, and I am faced with the horrid prospect of having to whittle the jagged remnants of a point down with either my fingernails (leading to splinters under the nail—wasn't that a method of torture at one time?), or with the alternately savage choice of using my teeth. Even if either scenario works in a timely fashion, the point I end up with is barely usable, and usually rather tenuous. I am human—limited and incomplete without technology.

The situation is comical at best, quite possibly life-threatening for the victim at worst. But it is that "scrolling through" of options, and the increasing stress that occurs as we eventually move closer toward our own bodies as a solution.[22] But on a larger, more complex scale, our inefficacy as human beings becomes most apparent in our inability to efficiently deal with information: to record (remember) it; to decode (understand) it; to manipulate it. In a world rendered as code, our bodies betray us in their inability to directly interface with that technologically codified information.

In a technologically advanced society (where the posthuman point of view would be most pronounced), what we take in with our senses is simply the topmost "layer" of experience. Beneath that are various iterations and levels of "code" that constitute experience itself (think of the accuracy of a medical diagnosis if all a doctor could do was look at you with only the naked eye, feel all manner of lumps and bumps without the aid of a biopsy, and listen to your heart without a stethoscope). Without technological systems, we are limited in what we can achieve with only our bodies—especially when we know that there are tools "out there" that can help us do what needs to be done.

Oedipa Maas is experiencing an epic version of this lack of apparatus and failure of interface. She also illustrates the *fear* involved in attempting to negotiate the boundaries between the human and technological other. Oedipa is afraid that if she does not successfully negotiate the boundary between herself and the Tristero, she will never be able to live up to her role as executrix of the Inverarity estate. What has become her defining characteristic in the text would be nullified by her own human shortcomings.

What offers us the deepest insight, however, into posthuman subjectivity is examining exactly what Oedipa is looking for in terms of interface itself. We must keep in mind that finding the right apparatus is, for Oedipa, a pre-condition for understanding the Tristero and thus executing the will. But from a reader's standpoint, that search for apparatus *is* the subject of the narrative itself. Thus, Oedipa is unaware of what a successful interface will bring her, other than insight. That interface will uncover something for her—something which, in her current state, she knows she cannot understand. Posthumanism does the same, especially if we look to Hayles's earlier statement regarding the present moment as a "critical juncture." The posthuman subjectivity we are waiting for would be an utter reconceptualization of subjectivity itself, one that we—as humans—cannot know. What artifact will satisfy our *need* for artifacts? For Oedipa, it is the Nefastis Machine.

The machine was designed to exploit the "Maxwell's Demon" theory as proposed by Scottish scientist Clerk Maxwell, who postulated a theory of thermodynamic perpetual motion that depends upon "a tiny intelligence," known as "Maxwell's Demon." In order to make the machine work, a "sensitive" was needed to concentrate on a picture of Maxwell that was printed on the front of the machine. When Oedipa eventually does meet Nefastis, he explains that the

Maxwell's Demon theory of entropy was the connecting point between both information theory and thermodynamics—two seemingly unrelated fields.[23] Sensitives who could make contact with the demon would then able to influence the placement of molecules in one of the chambers, causing one of the pistons to rise.

Note here that someone who can make contact with the machine is a "sensitive." While Haraway and Hayles never actually use the term, it is implied throughout both the "Cyborg Manifesto" and *How We Became Posthuman.* The posthuman/cyborg is someone who can be aware of (or sensitive to) his or her relationship with technology on every level, and achieve an understanding that allows his or her human awareness to be expanded in such a way that the site of interface itself is erased. This allows for an impossibly seamless, direct connection with the system itself, while still maintaining a human subjectivity.

The Nefastis machine is interesting in that it represents a *direct* connection with a technological system without any kind of tactile interface. All that the sensitive needed was concentration (a very human attribute). His or her awareness alone would be enough to effect a physical change on a technological system. Is this not the posthuman dream? It is a clean, non-invasive interface that requires no direct contact with the technological system, while still giving one the ability to bring about a change in the machine itself. It becomes more of a metaphysical connection than a human/machine interface, clean and ethereal.

The opportunity for direct contact with the "demon" within the machine becomes the embodiment of Oedipa's implied quest for the right apparatus. Sitting before the machine, she seeks out a connection:

> And there. At the top edge of what she could see: hadn't the right-hand piston moved, a fraction? She couldn't look directly, the instructions were to keep her eyes on Clerk Maxwell. Minutes passed, pistons remained frozen in place. High-pitched, cosmic voices issued from the TV set.[24]

At this moment, the conflict between the procedural parameters of interface and Oedipa's own "gut reactions" and physical limitations are most evident, and most clearly illustrates the limitations of a dream-scenario posthuman subjectivity. Even though Oedipa has made a connection with the larger technological system (the cosmic voice of the Tristero), she feels that she cannot make the necessary leap to get the machine itself work.

Posthuman subjectivity asks us to do the same thing as Oedipa Maas. We must "keep our eyes" on the boundary between us and the technological other, but not "look directly" at the results that occur in the system. Furthermore, the "results" that would occur would be imperceptible by our human senses. In order to achieve a posthuman subjectivity, we procedurally are forced to concentrate on the object of interface itself, rather than on "the world" that interface brings into being.

Concentrating on the Nefastis Machine as an object, Oedipa keeps herself from recognizing the significance of "cosmic voices" which have been singing to her since the start of the novel. The change she experienced was just on the verge of her perception, but at the very moment when she detected movement, she was *immediately* impeded by the "instructions" not to look directly at the machine itself. Oedipa is blocked by both procedure (which limits the scope of her gaze) and her own mistrust of her human senses. "Thinking" that she saw something move was not enough as *actually* seeing it. Oedipa downplays her own instincts in favor of empirical evidence. As the moment continues, she further downplays her own physicality:

> She had seen only a retinal twitch, a misfired nerve cell. Did the true sensitive see more? In her colon now she was afraid, growing more so, that nothing would happen. Why worry, she worried; Nefastis is a nut, forget it, a sincere nut. The true sensitive is one that can share in the man's hallucinations, that's all.[25]

Oedipa quickly attributes what she saw as a manifestation of her own human, physical shortcomings (misfired nerve cells and retinal twitches). Holding herself up to a model of technological results, she believes that she should have seen "more." When she does not live up to her own, technologically-inspired expectations, she feels a deep, visceral fear that there would be nothing to show for her efforts. Fear turns to doubt—not to the machine or the system—but toward Nefastis (the human aspect of the Nefastis Machine) himself. Oedipa further negates her abilities by thinking that even if she *were* a "true sensitive," she would only be sharing in a madman's hallucinations.

Oedipa is blind to the connections she makes through the Nefastis Machine, not because she's unable to see (or hear) them, but because she's actually looking for something else: an acknowledgement by the system *marked by her own ability to affect change in that system.* Oedipa wants to see results *on her own terms.* She wants to recognize herself—her own agency—in the system. If that piston had moved the way she wanted it move, it would have been a sign that the system acknowledged her for what she was. She would have reached out to the system—embraced it. The piston's movement would have been the system embracing her back, showing that the connection was there on Oedipa's own terms and that she was a true sensitive.

For the posthuman, posthuman subjectivity is a means of having it both ways, of achieving and interface with the machine by one's own (human) terms. It allows for a seamless interface where human agency is perfectly reflected in the technological system. What such a dream would produce would *not* be an expanded embodied awareness, but instead a perfect representation/ acknowledgement of humanity—a perfectly created other that could "know" our suffering.

But, for Oedipa, it was not to be. Immediately following her thoughts regarding the role of the "true sensitive," Oedipa continues:

How wonderful they [Nefastis's hallucinations] they might be to share. For fifteen minutes more she tried; repeating, if you are there, whatever you are, show yourself to me, I need you, show yourself. But nothing happened.

"I'm sorry," she called in, surprisingly, about to cry with frustration, her voice breaking. "It's no use."[26]

Oedipa's desperate pleading is, at its most basic, a desire for recognition by the machine—which for Oedipa—has come to represent the Tristero itself. She is, in terms of Scarry, attempting to "make herself available" to the system the only way she can. Very quickly, concentrating on the image of Clerk Maxwell transforms into a prayer to the machine (the apparatus of interface), and then eventually to the larger system of the Tristero. She has placed so much importance on this moment, that her own failure to make meaningful contact represents a failure on a much grander scale. Ironically, it is the Tristero which is making contact with her, but not on Oedipa's terms, thus, she cannot recognize its advances.

The prayer to the system also makes the Tristero seem like a sentient entity[27] which Oedipa herself has empowered by her own prayers to it. Oedipa's situation here poignantly illustrates what is at stake when we "surrender our interiors"[28] to a technological other. The failure Oedipa—and the aspiring posthuman—experience is the inability to remake ourselves into the image of the other. Without the proper apparatus, not only can we not remake ourselves in technology's image, we thus cannot enable technology "to enter and alter" ourselves.[29] Both Oedipa and the posthuman perform the same maneuver. Posthumanism starts out with the assumption that technology *is* the other, and a superior other at that. However, to salvage the "human" in light of this, Hayles attempts to reclaim the physicality of the human, while Haraway attempts to reclaim the tools by which the body is encoded, so that humans may take charge of their own inscription in the system.

As we have already seen, Oedipa has been repeatedly "encoded" by the Tristero. In her moment of prayer, she is not simply asking the Tristero to show itself, but she is also asking to see *herself*. Her prayer "If you are there, show yourself to me," could easily read, "If I am there, show myself to me." In her failure to "use" the Nefastis Machine effectively, she has failed in living out the cyborg ontology of Donna Haraway: she has not taken back the means by which she has been encoded.

Most importantly, however, Oedipa's prayer to the system is an act of submission to it; an acknowledgement that it is superior and capable of representing her without her consent. Is this not the silent admission present in posthumanism itself; the implied assumption to which Hayles herself cannot give voice? In order to be posthuman, we must, before anything else, submit to the system by admitting its superiority. The "embrace" that Haraway and Hayles long for is an attempt for control *after the fact*. Just as posthumanism as a discourse takes place after the point of interface between human and technological systems—without an exploration of what we, as humans, *need* from that system.

Indeed, what we want is to be more effective—to reach or "embodied awareness" as human beings. But what we need from technology is something else, and something more threatening. We need to be acknowledged by it. We need to know that it knows we're there. We need, as Scarry tells us, "to deprive [it] of the privilege of being inanimate."[30] This is the key to compatibility, and the ultimate goal of the posthuman—to be compatible with the world. To know that the external world can know *our* pain as humans. To know that the external world *can suffer with us.*

Oedipa Maas's search for apparatus illustrates the basic foundations for posthuman suffering. Her feelings of inadequacy that stem from her inability to understand information creates an ongoing cycle of inefficacy which she feels will only be lifted when she can complete her task. Unfortunately, completing her task depends upon her ability to understand that information.

Concluding Humanity: Giving Over the Narrative

Faced with this no-win scenario, Oedipa ultimately "defaults" to seeking out an end to it all. She seeks to *conclude*, rather than complete her journey. In Oedipa's mind, execution of her task would mean the *conclusion* of her task. That is to say, once she executes the will of Inverarity, she will have all the answers. In the technologically defined world of the Tristero, there is no conclusion—regardless of the conscious or unconscious attempts Oedipa enacts to invoke one. Instead, the Tristero is governed by more *technological* laws of *completion* (a "filling up," as opposed to an enclosing).

For Oedipa, the only semblance of a conclusion comes in a final, desperate call to one her "knights,"[31] to whom she tells the details of her entire journey: "She told him, quickly, using up no more than a minute, what she'd learned about the Tristero."[32] She begs the voice to tell her whether or not he too was implicated in the Tristero, and whether or not her initial meeting was "prearranged." Frustrated by his lack of a response, she declares, "They have saturated me . . . you can tell me." Oedipa's attempt to invoke a conclusion (by saying that she was "saturated" with information) is rendered useless by her almost immediate demand for yet *more* information; again, Oedipa's iteration of asking "what else?" Afterward, the voice declares, "It's too late," and hangs up. Ironically, her saturation *is* a technological completion. But her humanity demands a more narrative *conclusion* that she understands on her own terms. A technologically mediated completion cannot be represented in human terms.

One cannot underestimate the significance of this action in relation to posthumanism. Oedipa's recounting of her story into the phone is in keeping with her overall (posthuman) tendency to privilege technological systems, and now becomes the ultimate "submission" to the system. She literally "gives up her story" to the system—dictating her adventures *into and through* a technological artifact. She "gives up" (as in, *giving upward*) to the system itself. Although she feels most cut off from the system, she is—at this point—the closest to *literally* being subsumed back into it; losing herself completely in the system. She cannot take in any more. In "giving up" her story to the phone, she also gives up both her narrative standing and her faith in the relevancy of conclusions themselves:

> She stood between the public booth and the rented car, in the night, her isolation complete, and tried to face toward the sea. But she'd lost her bearings. She turned, pivoting on one stacked heel, could find no mountains either. As if there could be no barriers between herself and the land. San Narciso at that moment lost (the loss pure, instant, spherical, the sound of a stainless orchestral chime held among the starts and struck lightly), gave up its residue of uniqueness for her; became a name again, was assumed back into the American continuity of crust and mantle. Pierce Inverarity was really dead.[33]

In the physical space between the phone (a technological artifact and means of communication with the system) and the car (her technological means of navigation through the system), Oedipa cannot see beyond the parameters of her narrative (program). Here, Oedipa is in a state of loss. In "losing her bearings," she loses touch with the self-generated, defining boundaries which allowed her to determine her "place" in the world. San Narciso—literally representing the possibility of a sanctified ego while simultaneously representing the possibility of the lack of an ego—is itself lost.

At this moment, the reader is given a necessarily momentary glimpse of how a total posthuman subjectivity might manifest itself. Pynchon illustrates what *total* interface with the system would/does require, and in so doing, shows the impossibility of sustaining such a state for any length of time beyond an almost imperceptible flicker. This kind of interface is equivalent to a *technological* completion; that is to say, a total integration with the system which necessarily nullifies the *need* for interface.[34]

Oedipa *never* crossed any boundary, nor did she transcend from her narrative, system, tapestry, or whatever other metaphor one can come up with. There is no transcendence here; her "assumption" back into her self-reflexive tapestry is a gesture toward the impossibility of "true" transcendence through technological means. She is, for all intents and purposes, where she has always been—the executrix of the will of Pierce Inverarity. The execution of her program *does not* bring her a conclusion, at least according to the final line of the novel: "Oedipa settled back, to await the crying of lot 49," indicating that the story is about to begin again. The final piece of information is held indefinitely in a state of suspension, perhaps preparing Oedipa for the next iteration of the story itself.

Oedipa's inability to knowingly gain a recognizable compatibility with "the system" and her perceived alienation from it is proof of her obsolescence. Her feelings of inadequacy were a direct result of her attempts to hold herself up to a technological standard of functionality and equate the achievement of any kind of interface as a means to an end. Her attempts at interface were informed by largely pre-conceived notions of efficacy as defined by her own poorly-understood theories of thermodynamics and information. She felt that the ability to "project a world" would necessarily give her control over that world.

Oedipa Maas's journey in *The Crying of Lot 49* illustrates some of the unspoken difficulties inherent in achieving a literal posthuman subjectivity. Even though Oedipa has been "activated" and is faced with vast amounts of information regarding the extent of the Tristero, she is plagued by feelings of inadequacy. If only she could find the right apparatus by which to engage the system of information she's faced with, she could begin her quest and achieve her task.

Posthumanism places us in the same position as Oedipa Maas, poised on the verge of achieving full "embodied awareness," but only on the condition that we find the right technological apparatus to bring us to that point. Oedipa repeatedly attempts to embrace the Tristero, but her attempts at interface fail each time. No apparatus brings her the direct contact she desires. Ironically, she has already been implicated and inscribed in the Tristero itself, but she is both unwilling and unable to accept the system's representations of her. She needs acknowledgements in terms *she* can understand.

While we have been told that the posthuman is already among us, it is more accurate to say that *the desire to be posthuman* is already among us. Although literal posthuman subjectivity implies a complete transcendence of humanity itself, what posthuman discourse is actually seeking is a perfectly technified "other" who can perfectly articulate the pain of the human condition.

Oedipa inhabits the space before posthuman subjectivity is actually reached, where the physicality of the body acts as an insurmountable boundary: no matter how hard we try to make ourselves more compatible with our technological systems, allowing the technologically superior other to "enter and alter" us is easier said than done. In a world more frequently characterized as a manifestation of code, where experience itself is nothing more than the proprietary, flawed interface that human beings utilize in an attempt to deal with information, an inability to deal with information alienates us from the world itself. The ultimate goal of the posthuman is to be as compatible as possible with the information that makes up the external world. We want the world to acknowledge our suffering, and to suffer with us.

Notes

1. In the novel, The Tristero, (also Trystero), was one of two competing private mail delivery companies in the 1700s. It continues to exist in Oedipa's world as an underground mail delivery system. As the novel progresses, however, the Tristero becomes woven into Oedipa's life to such an extent that Oedipa begins to believe that it has an intrinsic power over her.

2. Thomas Pynchon, *The Crying of Lot 49* (New York: Harper & Row, 1966), 21.

3. David Seed, *The Fictional Labyrinths of Thomas Pynchon* (London: MacMillan Press, 1988), 124.

4. Patrick O'Donnell, "Engendering Paranoia in Contemporary Narrative," *Boundary 2* 19.1 (1992), 190-92.

5. O'Donnell, "Engendering Paranoia," 190.

6. Thomas Hill Schaub, *Pynchon: The Voice of Ambiguity* (Urbana: The University of Illinois Press, 1981), 31.

7. Dwight Eddins, *The Gnostic Pynchon* (Bloomington: Indiana University Press, 1990), 91.

8. Alan Wilde, *Middle Grounds: Studies in Contemporary American Fiction* (Philadelphia: The University of Pennsylvania Press, 1987), 99.

9. Eddins, *Gnostic Pynchon*, 13.

10. Pynchon, *Crying*, 22.

11. Pynchon, *Crying*, 37.

12. Pynchon, *Crying*, 26.

13. Pynchon, *Crying*, 79.

14. Scarry, *Body in Pain*, 128.

15. Pynchon, *Crying*, 82.

16. A "Pynchonism" of "stelliform"—star shaped.

17. Hayles, *Posthuman*, 2.

18. Hayles, *Posthuman*, 2.

19. Hayles and Haraway tend to engage the human/technological with what can only be called a binary complexity. That is to say, posthumanism/cyborg subjectivity is a series of either/or situations. Either you are posthuman or you aren't. If you are posthuman, then you are either an informed posthuman or an ignorant posthuman. If ignorant, then you are either the victim of a grafted liberal humanism, or you are simply unaware that you already are posthuman. Ironically, the binaries actually begin to read like a BASIC computer program (If x = y, then goto z).

20. Hayles, *Posthuman*, 5.

21. It was after the Second World War, when guidance systems of missiles and complex computers were being built, that the concept of "information" began its transformation and "disembodiment." (See endnote five in the introduction regarding the Macy Conferences).

22. Another pertinent example would be the student/writer/scholar who composes exclusively on a computer. The word processor program becomes corrupt, he or she moves onto a simple "wordpad" program. If the computer itself crashes or the power goes down, they are left with either a voice recorder or—horror of horrors—pad and pencil. At which point we can ultimately return to the scenario above.

23. According to Nefastis, "The sensitive must receive that staggering set of energies, and feed back something like the same quantity of information." Pynchon, *Crying*, 105.

24. Pynchon, *Crying*, 107.

25. Pynchon, *Crying*, 107.

26. Pynchon, *Crying*, 107.

27. For characterizations of the Tristero as a sentient entity, see Eddins, 94-5; and John Johnston, "Toward the Schizo-Text: Paranoia as Semiotic Regime in *The Crying of Lot 49*" in *New Essays on* The Crying of Lot 49 (New York: Cambridge UP, 1991), 67.

28. Scarry, *Body in Pain*, 204.

29. Scarry, *Body in Pain*, 197.

30. Scarry, *Body in Pain*, 285.

31. The knight in question is member of "Inamorato Anonymous" whom Oedipa meets in the "Greek Way" bar earlier in the novel. This nameless character gives her

critical information regarding the history of the Tristero and how to use the WASTE mail system.

32. Pynchon, *Crying*, 176-77.

33. Pynchon, *Crying*, 177.

34. From a humanist standpoint, achieving this kind of integration would erase that human by eradicating the human point of view. Thus, any "real interface" would be momentary, instant, and all-encompassing.

Chapter Three

Humanism Through Technology: Situating the Subject in Hayles and Haraway

If we are to engage posthumanism as a mode of inquiry, it is necessary to understand its relationship to humanism, especially in terms of human subjectivity. In his 2003 article "Theorizing Posthumanism," Neil Badmington better articulates the call for a critical posthumanism that is put forth in both Hayles and Haraway through a closer examination of the Cartesian subject in light of technological development. The article also attempts to illustrate the implications of an uncritical, or "complacent" reinscription of the humanist paradigm in a technological idiom.

Badmington characterizes the nightmare scenarios, which both Hayles and Haraway seem to fear, as "complacent posthumanism," marked by "the seemingly posthumanist desire to download consciousness into a gleaming digital environment [which] is itself downloaded from the distinctly humanist matrix of Cartesian Dualism."[1] Like Hayles and Haraway, Badmington maintains that complacent posthumanism adheres to the humanist idea that consciousness (as an act of cognition) is the true "essence" of the human, and that the body is ultimately a prosthesis of consciousness which can—and will—eventually be shed.

Badmington picks up where Hayles and Haraway leave off by directly engaging the humanist subject, maintaining that posthumanism is not a "replacement" for humanism, nor is it an opportunity to forget or cast off humanism all together. Instead, it is a means by which to re-think humanism from within. Borrowing heavily from Lyotard and Freud, Badmington sees posthumanism as a "working through" or "anamnesis" of humanism.[2] In this manner, critical posthumanism becomes a method by which we can deconstruct the humanist subject by using the same "language" that liberal humanism uses to define itself.

Under posthumanism, the "language" in question is one which is based on the assumption that information and code—quantities without substance—permeate and constitute everything. In the same fashion as Haraway's cyborg, we must take back the "coding" lest it reproduce the same self/other dichotomies (and their negative effects) which arise in Cartesian humanism. For Badmington, posthumanism is *not* an absolute break with humanism, nor does it simply repackage the humanist subject. "If the version of posthumanism that I am trying to develop here repeats humanism, it does so *in a certain way* and with a view to

53

the deconstruction of anthropomorphic thought."[3] For Badmington, posthumanism is a methodology by which to engage humanism in light of technological development.

What Badmington does here is indeed an attempt at the kind of informed, critical posthumanism which Hayles calls for in *How We Became Posthuman*, and provides one of the first explorations of the humanist roots of posthumanism from which Hayles shies away. Most interesting is the invocation of anamnesis as a better way to situate posthumanism's humanist roots. Badmington's choice of a partially psychoanalytic approach implies that posthumanism itself evolved as a reaction to the trauma brought about by the humanist subject's ongoing attempts to redefine itself and remain relevant in light of humanity's ongoing technological development. In so doing, however, he actually reinforces several aspects of the liberal humanist subject. By choosing anamnesis as a means to "recollect" or uncover certain forgotten connections which have occurred as humanism "slips into the posthuman," Badmington attempts to re-establish and emphasize the very narrative quality of human subjectivity (a quality on which posthumanism remains conspicuously silent).

This is an important area to explore, because the posthuman suffering which we have witnessed through Oedipa Maas (and will witness in *White Noise* and *AI: Artificial Intelligence*) is most often characterized by the protagonists' attempts to rectify their narrative desire to *conclude* with their technological aspirations to *complete*. They want to be more like what they perceive as a superior, technological other. However, these characters cannot find the apparatus to help them achieve their goals, rendering a technological "completion" impossible. Left with no satisfactory means of interface, they "default" to seeking a narrative conclusion—believing that somehow *invoking* a conclusion (rather than achieving a completion) will give them the answers to the questions for which they do not have the "apparatus" to ask in the first place. Instead of seeking answers—the objects of their quests—each character is instead looking for the right apparatus with which to frame the questions. The object of the interface becomes the objective of the quest itself.

In realistic terms, the pattern outlined above manifests itself as a posthuman suffering, which has at its core a general faith in what we perceive as superior technological systems. While each system we use (a computer, an ATM, an e-mail client) addresses a specific need and fulfills a certain purpose, often the needs we are attempting to satisfy run much deeper than simply needing to send an e-mail or get cash. Our technological systems have come to *represent* a deeper need for acknowledgment and efficacy in an increasingly technified world. The main difficulty we face is that our very human, narrative means of enframing the world often comes into direct conflict with the technological models to which we increasingly aspire. Posthumanism as discourse grows out of that conflict, and also has the means to address it by examining the site(s) of interface itself. At times, however, it chooses not to.

While the previous chapter explored the basic assumptions and central ideas of posthumanism, the present chapter will uncover the deeper, less obvious philosophical and psychological foundations which posthumanism seems to have "forgotten." Specifically, we will examine the relationship between Cartesian humanism and posthumanism, especially the aspects of the former to which the latter still tenaciously clings. Posthumanism's failure to come to terms with its own reliance on the "other" has transformed technology itself into an object of faith. We shall also see that Freud himself furthered a more formalized system of technological faith almost a century prior to postwar theories of cybernetics. He too had the same difficulties in rectifying technological examples of completion with more narrative manifestations of conclusions that posthumanism has. Finally, Don DeLillo's *White Noise* will serve to illustrate these difficulties in more contemporary and literary terms. Going a step further than Oedipa Maas, Jack Gladney starts out with complete faith in technology, until he is alienated from his defining data. Sensing a "plot" at work, Jack attempts to invoke a conclusion to achieve both a narrative end *and* a more technified *completion* to his story.

The Subject and Cartesian Roots

Badmington suggests that "humanism is forever rewriting itself as posthumanism"[4] by strategically relocating the "subject" so that it can remain viable amid changing concepts of information, embodiment, and physicality. We can say that the Cartesian subject is being "recapitulated" in reaction to technological advancement, being made more compatible not only with information, but with more contemporary theories of information and information transfer. We must recall here the posthumanist assumption that the body is a prosthesis for consciousness. Here, Badmington makes the type of insightful advances for which Hayles's critical posthumanism is looking. However, he eventually falls short when he attempts to engage posthumanism's own conclusions. It is necessary to take a brief detour through Cartesian humanism to understand how the subject is so easily separated from its human body before we can understand exactly why Badmington falls short.

In Cartesian humanism, the human ability to reason is what separates us from animals, and the "power of judging well and distinguishing the true from the false" is present and "naturally equal in all men."[5] Humanity's capacity for epistemological deduction fuses metaphysics with ontology to bring Descartes to his (in)famous axiom *Cogito ergo Sum* (commonly translated as "I think therefore I am"). The rational mind is the at the center of what it means to be human, and that mind is "entirely distinct from the body."[6] Descartes' belief that he could pretend that he had no body, but could *not* pretend that he did not exist, proved to him that existence did not require material presence: "I knew from there that I was a substance whose whole essence or nature is solely to think, and who, in order to exist, does not require any place, or depend on any material thing."[7]

Badmington points out that even though four years later, in *Meditations*, Descartes did admit the mind and body were linked, he still reaffirmed "a fundamental dualism" between them.[8] When Descartes considered himself as a thinking being, he found that he was "unable to distinguish any parts within [him]self," and that he considered himself to be "something quite single and complete."[9] Descartes continues: "Although the whole mind seems to be united to the whole body, I recognize that if a foot or arm or any other part of the body is cut off, nothing has thereby been taken away from the mind."[10] While the ability to think was dependent upon the physicality of one's embodied mind, the ability to *recognize* one's own ability to think seemed, to Descartes at least, to be completely separate from the body. The human being was "completely known, knowable, and present in the very being that is engaged in the meditation on what it means to be human."[11] This "disembodiment" of consciousness becomes a serious issue in posthumanism, primarily because it supports the more complacent idea that the consciousness can be compartmentalized, or "lifted out" of the body. Critical posthumanism, in turn, (especially in terms of Hayles and Haraway) attempts to re-emphasize the importance of embodiment, characterizing the body as the proprietary interface with the world, and recognizing that the way in which we perceive the world is dictated by our own physical, biological systems of perception.

However, there is still an aspect of Cartesian humanism upon which critical posthumanism relies most heavily: the importance of self-recognition. It is *imperative* to Hayles's posthuman and Haraway's cyborg that each *recognize itself* as such. Each must be able to be aware of the boundaries between itself and its technological systems (an iteration of the self/other dichotomy) in order to mediate more effectively those boundaries more effectively. No matter how negatively each characterizes the "liberal humanist subject," no matter how eagerly each seeks to escape its "domination," as long as posthumanist discourse relies upon human awareness as a defining characteristic, it will be dependent upon an aspect of humanist subjectivity. Like Haraway's cyborg bastard-child, posthumanism cannot escape its "biological parents" of subjectivity and the need for a cohesive self in light of the "other." However subjectivity is recapitulated, it remains unshakably Cartesian in its reliance upon self-awareness.

It is indeed a difficult fence for posthumanism to straddle, and it does so by making the very clear distinction between the nightmare and dream scenarios already outlined in the previous chapter. The reinscription of the humanist subject in complacent posthumanism occurs when the consciousness is considered completely independent of biological embodiment: where simply having a viable point of view—a notion of self—would be enough to call ourselves "human," even in the most bizarre, science-fiction inspired manifestations. The fact that I could refer to myself, to think in the "I am" would mean that I was human in the Cartesian sense, even if "I" were a brain in a jar attached to some kind of robot-spider body. The body in which "I" was housed wouldn't matter, as long as there was a viable self inhabiting it. By contrast, the critical posthuman, living out its dream scenario, would fundamentally *know* (being an informed posthuman) that human perception and self-awareness rely upon the physical and biological processes of the human brain, and be "fully aware" of the nature of the boundary between the self and technological other in a transcendent way. Furthermore, human experience is made unique by our own physical sensory interface with the world.

But there is a more subtle subtext at work here, which permeates even the most critical of posthuman dreams. The self, whether human or posthuman, is epistemologically legitimized by being "knowable." Its existence is contingent upon its ability to recognize itself in relation to an "other" which it can willingly and knowingly embrace. In posthumanism, that other is technology. Furthermore, for the posthuman, if consciousness is a pattern of information, then one's degree of self-awareness correlates to one's ability to handle, decode, and be compatible with that information. The posthuman concedes that without the supplement of technology, the human is limited in its physicality. Thus, the only way to achieve a greater compatibility with information (both the information that constitutes the human itself and the world we inhabit) is through more advanced technological systems. In posthumanism, intrinsically *knowing* the self is contingent upon the supplement of the technological other. We cannot know ourselves—nor can we reach our full embodied, human potential—without some kind of technological other to help us "re-connect" with ourselves. Posthuman suffering does not stem from the fact that it relies on the technological "other"; it arises from the assumption that we need the technological "other" to *know ourselves*.

As we have already established, the posthuman dreams of Haraway and Hayles are dependent upon understanding the relationships between human beings and technology, and constructively using technology to expand our embodied awareness. Technology in this sense not only encompasses the artifacts and systems that "extend our reach," so to speak, but also allows us to understand the workings of our biological bodies so that we can more easily, less invasively, incorporate technological systems into our-"selves" (in both a literal and Cartesian sense). This, of course, can be achieved only through an ongoing uncovering, decoding, and understanding of the "information" of which we are constituted. The "fully embodied posthuman" would be the *complete* human—one who has used technology to achieve a total compatibility with the information of experience that is available to it.

Under Hayles' reconceptualization of information—specifically the idea that all material things are made up of "bodiless information"—the desire to uncover, unlock, and control the information that makes up the human being starts to become a paradoxical and circular moral imperative: our survival and evolution as human beings depend upon our understanding of, and our ability to *interface* with the very information of which we are constituted. We are reminded here of Elaine Scarry's contention that in an attempt to make ourselves more "available" to a superior system (in her case, a deity; in our case, technology), humans attempt to "turn themselves inside out." The dynamic here is similar in that posthuman discourse characterizes the internal working of the body as both a processing—and literal expression—of information itself.[12] Everything is comprised of information, and we, as human beings, are simply a different expression of information. The better we can read (and manipulate) our own data, the better we can integrate with the data that constitute every aspect of the world we inhabit. Ultimately, critical posthumanism *does not* believe that it is necessary to forgo the physical body to do this, but a technological supplement of some kind *is* necessary in order for us to have as much information as possible (about ourselves, about the world) available to us. Thus, we may eventually be able to learn how to process and manipulate the information within and around us *without the aid of a technological apparatus.*

This opens up a very important, albeit unspoken, posthuman "reality": the more information we uncover regarding how the human-as-system works, the better our tools to uncover that information become. The better those tools become, the more we realize that there is even more information to uncovered. The prospect of "knowing ourselves" becomes locked into the technological means by which we enact such knowing. In order to "know" ourselves, we must create better technology to uncover more information. And in order to know ourselves better, we must be as compatible with that technology (and the information it uncovers) as possible. Without technology, we are at a distinct disadvantage in reaching our human potential.

What posthumanism does *not* address, however, is that with technology, we are faced with the possibility that there is *always more information to be uncovered.* The end point, logically, would be a saturation of information, a total completion or "filling up" of all there is to know. Paradoxically, saturation implies the satisfaction of the need for information, a state which would preclude the human condition itself.

This is where a dream-scenario posthuman "directive" begins to reveal itself. Technological systems, for critical posthumanism, *must* remain as a separate other so that the embodied human—once "completed"—can achieve a state where he or she no longer *needs* technology in order to participate fully and unhindered in the infinite amount of information which the world, and indeed the universe itself, has to offer. It would be an unlimited exchange with not only the universe, but with other posthumans as well. Again, we return to Scarry and the idea that we suffer because we cannot *know* another's pain. Furthermore, through analogical verification, we bestow human qualities on the inanimate world in order ultimately to have the world acknowledge and reflect our physical, metaphysical, and ontological pain. How this would be possible without forgoing the human body altogether is the stuff of science fiction, but the dream is often represented in various literary and cinematic examples when an "enlightened" humanity achieves a state where technology aides in human development/evolution until human beings willingly abandon all material and technological trappings for a more transcendent, or ethereal state.[13]

Critical posthumanism maintains that if we were to be complacent in our application of the posthuman paradigm, and allow ourselves to attempt to "upload" our consciousness into a machine rather than be aware (or even "celebrate") the finitude of our human bodies, it would threaten human subjectivity by rearticulating the most human aspect of humanity—the consciousness itself. We would be integrated with technology in such a way that we could no longer be aware of the boundaries between ourselves and our technological systems—threatening us with dissolution. Instead of full embodied awareness, we would instead achieve a sort of human/machine hybrid subjectivity, which would merge human and artificial "being" into a completely other teleology. Ironically, it is critical posthumanism more than its complacent counterpart which wants to protect human subjectivity as per Cartesian humanism.

Protecting the Subject: The Rise of Complacent Posthumanism

The fear of a literal dissolution of the subject brought about through *technological means* is one which goes hand-in-hand with postwar research in cybernetics, especially in light of such swiftly moving technological development of computers and digital systems in general.[14] Descartes *did* anticipate the more far-reaching possibilities of technology. While he did not foresee the advent of the cyborg or the possibility of downloading one's consciousness into a different body, he did envision the possibility of "mechanical" reproductions of animals and humans. However "Descartes asserts his anthropocentrism on the grounds that it would be impossible for a machine to possess enough different organs to enable it to respond to the infinite unpredictability of everyday life."[15] Given the fact that Descartes was writing in the first half of the seventeenth century, it was inconceivable to him that anything artificial might so closely mimic the qualities of a biological human being.

The difficulty here—as Badmington points out—is that we are quickly approaching the "fantastic scenario" where it might be possible for a machine to be constructed with as much (and possibly more) complexity than a human being, and that the unique interplay of its systems might mimic, reproduce, or replicate a human so well that it could be impossible to tell the difference between the artificial human and the inhuman. This, in turn, would negate the validity of Cartesian humanism "*according to the letter of Descartes' own argument.*"[16]

Faced with the possible (and for some, inevitable) rise of the artificial human, or, in an apt term coined by Badmington, the "simulcarian," humanism complacently "slips into posthumanism"[17] and protects the validity of the subject by allowing for the possibility that cognition can occur in a non-biological substrate. As technology advances, it becomes clear how complacent posthumanism might abandon the human body altogether and seek out a method by which the Cartesian subject is retained, or, more correctly, kept "special" in light of the possibility of a system-for-system, organ-for-organ replicant of the human being. For traditional Cartesian humanism, embodiment did not matter simply because the possibility of an artificial body was not even close to a reality.

Complacent posthumanism, faced with this reality, needed to re-emphasize the seat of humanity in the rational mind, *but de-emphasize the materiality of the embodied mind* in order to privilege cognition as the true hallmark of humanity. Complacent posthumanism thus is characterized by Badmington as humanism's "replacement," or a modernized, technified "humanism 2.0." And it is this outlook that makes possible the nightmare scenarios put forward by Hayles and Haraway, raising the possibility that humans might actively seek ways to abandon their bodies, "trading up" for artificial bodies. The nightmare scenario here is that willingly forgoing the "uniqueness" of our present embodiment before we have realized its full potential might cause us to reinscribe the same human fears and flaws into a more powerful, less limited body. Again, how transcending the need for technology itself would nullify what Hayles and Haraway view as liberal humanism's "politics of domination" is never fully addressed. It becomes more a question of faith than anything else that a body unburdened by the need for technology would somehow be "cleaner," more ethereal, and free of the very limitations which created the need for technology in the first place.

What complacent and critical posthumanism *do* have in common is a reliance upon the subject itself. Complacent posthumanism seeks simply to re-cast the subject (upload the consciousness) into a new body. Critical posthumanism claims a higher, more theoretical purpose, seeking to rethink and *improve subjectivity through technology*; but despite all of its theory, it still relies on a technological "other" against which it can reflect a point-of-view cohesive enough to recognize itself. From this perspective, the main difference between the two approaches lies in the characterization of the interface as either a grafting (a physical integration with technology) or an embrace (a "taking in" with the option/intent of letting go). But each relies upon the tangibility of the artificial, technological "other" to make it work.

Badmington's approach mirrors critical posthumanism's dual purpose, to "work through" humanism, and then strive for a mode of being which takes into account the biological human's limited embodiment. It seeks out a more informed compatibility with the material world, setting up the possibilities of extended *embodied* awareness by utilizing technological systems as tool, not a replacement, for the human body. True critical posthumanism, in Badmington's view, should not abandon the human, "tak[ing] the form of a critical practice that occurs *inside* humanism, consisting not of the wake but the working-through of humanist discourse."[18]

Here, Badmington implies that critical posthumanism is a transitional zone (or middle state) between humanism and what could amount to a mode of being so different from our own that it literally *cannot be conceived of* as long as we remain incomplete, held back from our potential by our current inability to handle information as effectively as possible. Full embodied awareness necessarily depends upon technology for its "becoming." Like Hayles and Haraway before him, Badmington becomes rather vague regarding the possibilities of a fully embodied human, and turns to somewhat phenomenological language to describe the possibilities that posthumanism precedes: "I think that questioning humanism—posthumanism itself—begins to build ways for being different in the future. 'We' have nothing to lose but 'our'selves."[19]

Ultimately, an informed posthuman is the only one who will be ready for evolution/transcendence. If we are not informed, we will surely lose ourselves. "Taking responsibility" for our information emerges as a repeated theme in posthumanism, placing various degrees of importance on the means by which we are to manipulate—or be manipulated by—information. However, with such a directive, the fundamental assumption is that if we take responsibility for information, it will necessarily bring about control.

Posthumanism concedes that the only way to get information in hand is through a technological other, characterizing human beings as incomplete. But the unspoken implication is that there is some kind of "complete" version of the human which can be attained. This concession, however, is problematic in that the technologically-inspired concept of completion posthumanism looks toward is not completion at all; it is merely a conclusion (and a narrative one at that). Posthumanism assumes that there is a set quantity of information that needs to be revealed/acquired/understood in order for us to reach a technologically-inspired potential. The "completion" posthumanism seems to be striving for is an artificial one—a concept of completion created as a goal to be reached. Once reached, then the transcendent, completed human could "move on" to some other "next level" of existence. True completion would mean a total, unknowable dissolution; or an "inhuman" subjectivity, not bound by the rules of biology or physics.

Posthumanism's limitation is that it relies too heavily on the supplemental aspect of technology itself. If we look carefully at Hayles's and Scarry's posthuman dreams, we find that what they are really aspiring to is a *constant striving to be more human*, rather than *achieving* full humanity. Whether it's "celebrating our finitude" or taking responsibility for the tools of inscription, each approach strives for what it believes is a transcendence via the *addition* of technology, assuming that our need for technology in the first place arises from our own feelings of inefficacy and loss. Even Badmington, at his most critical, is still *aspiring* toward a technologically-mediated transcendence achieved via a human embrace of technology.

What then, is the alternative? Badmington (and even Hayles and Haraway themselves) characterize critical posthumanism as a methodology, or a means to improve our relationship with technology. And each briefly "flashes" on the fact that the utilization of technology is an inextricable part of being human and how we come to know the world. They each seem to conclude with the general sense that technology has become—or is becoming—a human ontology. By starting out with the assumption that technology is an "other" (and a superior one at that), each approach limits itself, somewhat blinded to the significance of the connection between human and technological other that has always existed.

The connection I am speaking of here requires us to *begin* where the assumptions of critical posthumanism *end*. If we begin with the assumption that technology *is* an intrinsic aspect of human ontology—that an integral part of our humanity is to take in the world (and itself) *technologically*, regardless of the time period or level of technological advancement we have reached—we can better address some of the deeper issues that posthumanism raises. If we look at technology as the *process* by which negotiate the boundary between self and other, we will be better able to understand our humanity in a world where the objects of technology seem to be eroding our human efficacy. For this, we must turn to more theoretical texts.

A Heideggerian Pause:
The Essence of Technology

Heidegger's essay, "The Question Concerning Technology," investigates the intricate relationship between humans and technology, and with the atomic age in mind, cautions us to be mindful of our technological advance as a species. Like posthumanism, "The Question Concerning Technology" envisions both dream and nightmare scenarios based on how "informed" our relationship with technology is. Furthermore, Heidegger anticipates posthumanism's reliance on a reconceptualization of information in his discussion of the "standing reserve" which is parallel—if not interchangeable—with more contemporary ideas of information and coding.

Heidegger, however, begins where posthumanism ends—articulating the idea that technology is the defining aspect of literally *being* human. Heidegger sees the essence of technology not as a separate entity that will enable us to understand the world better, but as an epistemology: technology is (and has always been) the manner in which we, as humans, apprehend—or "enframe"—the world. Technology is linked to humanity on the deepest level, in the space where the humanist self-other distinction is first formulated. For Heidegger, "technology is a way of revealing" which can ultimately lead to "truth."[20] In "The Question Concerning Technology," Heidegger wishes, above all, that we attempt to discover the "essence" of technology,[21] so that we may better understand our relationship to it. In contrast to posthumanism, Heidegger investigates this relationship in the space of interface itself, rather than *after* the connection has already been made.

To do this, Heidegger attempts to draw a clear line between the instrumentality of technology (in terms of its physical artifacts and systems) and the essence of technology (what technology *means*, what it *is* phenomenologically, and how it "*comes to presence*").[22] We cannot underestimate the importance of this distinction, because it allows Heidegger to re-emphasize the human as ultimately responsible for every aspect of technology, rather than unwittingly place technology as a superior other. The concepts of technology's instrumentality and its essence are very different, but technology's instrumentality has the potential to *overshadow* any investigation of its essence. This overshadowing is, I believe, what has occurred in critical posthumanism. Critical posthumanism's limitations occur because it has yet to make a similar distinction between technology as an object and technology as a method of knowing the world.

Heidegger states, "the essence of technology is by no means technological. Thus we shall never experience our relationship to the essence of technology so long as we merely conceive and push forward the technological, put up with it, or evade it."[23] Note here how Heidegger immediately characterizes our relationship to technology from a more phenomenological viewpoint as an "experience" rather than as a more posthuman "awareness" of the boundaries. Experience implies a more direct involvement, whereas an awareness of boundaries implies a witnessing that requires a separation of some kind. For Heidegger, an uncritical approach—one that sees technology as merely a means to an end or a system by which we can exploit natural resources (including humanity) for our own gain—only serves to pull us further away from the essence which Heidegger will come to identify.

Much like the temptation of Badmington's "complacent posthumanism," Heidegger maintains that "regarding technology as something neutral . . . makes us utterly blind to the essence of technology."[24] Although critical posthumanism may not view technology as "neutral," it generally does view it and its systems—without distinction—as a separate other. Objectifying technology as merely a tool to be wielded reinforces the idea that technology is something separate from us, rather than bringing us closer to an understanding of how technology is actually an integral aspect of human self-perception, and ultimately for human be-ing itself. For Heidegger, the instrumentality of technology is necessary to our day-to-day survival, but because of its utter ubiquity in our lives, it can also distract and stand in the way of a more philosophical investigation of technology's essence.

Ultimately, the instrumentally-dominated view is predicated on a desire to master technology, and to create increasingly complex systems of control to enforce that mastery and bring us into a better (read, *more compatible*) relationship with technology.

> The instrumental conception of technology conditions every attempt to bring man into the right relation to technology. Everything depends on our manipulating technology in the proper manner as a means. We will, as we say, "get" technology "spiritually in hand." We will master it. The will to mastery becomes all the more urgent the more technology threatens to slip from human control.[25]

Posthumanism itself is actually a manifestation of the "will to mastery" as Heidegger points out. Our attempts to embrace it, whether critically or uncritically, grow as we increasingly perceive the threat of technology slipping from human control. The threat actually becomes greater as our technological systems become more complex, as skill is continually built into those technological systems and out of the human (as Scarry outlines). In our desire to "get technology in hand," we run the risk of actually distancing ourselves from the essence of technology: what Heidegger believes is a *human* act of *bringing forth*. The essence of technology is a way of knowing, something which remains undeveloped at the heart of critical posthumanism. Even though critical posthumanism does momentarily consider technology as an epistemology, it does so at an instrumentally-inspired distance, linking authentic understanding (of the human, of technology, and of posthumanism itself) by approaching technology as an other.

Bringing Forth:
The Silversmith, the Chalice, and the
Inescapable Potentiality of the World

"The Question Concerning Technology" is predicated on the notion that technology is how we come to know the world; not in terms of how the scientific instruments reveal information regarding the various constitutive materials and processes of the world, but in terms of the process of how humans bring objects into being. Heidegger himself gives us the most succinct of examples.

A silversmith who crafts a silver chalice brings that chalice into being by taking the raw materials necessary, combining them, and then shaping them according to the context by which the chalice will be used. The chalice has been defined by the boundaries of both its physical material and its potential use. Most importantly, however, the bringing into existence of the chalice is dependent on the silversmith, who was responsible for bringing all the aspects of its "chaliceness" together. Responsibility here is more specifically articulated than it is in critical posthumanism. It is more "active" and teleological in Heidegger's model, and is asserted during the process of creation, rather than after the making of the artifact has taken place.

While the silversmith did not create the silver or even the concept of the chalice itself, he *did* create that specific chalice by bringing the various elemental "causes" together. In this manner, the silversmith is what "brings forth" and is responsible for the chalice. The chalice owes its bringing forth to the silversmith, because it cannot bring *itself* forth.[26] The implication here is that we are "masters" of our technology when we bring something forth, and are engaged in an act of creation rather than an act of interpretation or classification that is inherent in handling information as *data*.

In Heidegger's example, the human has used technology to bring forth—to *reveal*—the chalice; a chalice that will be used for a specific purpose (as a drinking vessel, or as part of some religious rite, or as a work of art, or any combination therein). What is significant here is the importance Heidegger places on the connection between the human and the object that is brought into being. This object not only serves a specific purpose in the physical world, but it also represents an "exchange" or interface with the world. Human efficacy is at its strongest in direct, purposeful, physical interaction. The chalice is "brought into" the world so that it may be "taken in" and experienced by its human creator (and others as well). The silversmith has brought something into being which both exists, and gives testimony to his existence.

We are reminded here of Scarry's work regarding technology as a means of human expression, and how that expression actually works to allow us to "take in" the world around us:

> What gradually becomes visible ... is the process by which a made world of culture acquires the characteristics of "reality," the process of perception that allows invented ideas, beliefs, and made objects to be accepted and entered into as though they had the same ontological status as the naturally given world. Once the made world is in place, it will have acquired the legitimate forms of "substantiation" that are familiar to us. That an invented thing is "real" will be ascertainable by the immediate apprehensible fact of itself ... [it] has a materialized existence that is confirmable by vision, touch, hearing, smell; its reality is accessible to all senses; its existence is thus confirmed within the bodies of the observers themselves.[27]

In Scarry's articulation of the actual process of creating which Heidegger presents, we can see exactly how integral a technological ontology is in creating a relationship with the physical world. Technology becomes the means by which we bridge the gap between self and other. The act of creation here that Heidegger and Scarry outline emphasizes a more direct connection between technology and human subjectivity than posthumanism seems to acknowledge. Furthermore, what is created is immediately accessible by the senses, and does not need some kind of supplemental instrumental apparatus to be experienced.

But what of more contemporary notions of technology? How relevant is Heidegger's chalice and silversmith to the data-sensitive technology of our own "digital" age, and/or regarding technologies which modern physical sciences have obviously helped develop? Heidegger anticipates an objection here regarding the difference between the work of a craftsman and "modern machine-powered technology."[28] Heidegger makes the case that "modern technology" presents itself differently than "older technologies," because modern technology is linked to putting science, and other instruments of technology *to use*. It uses various instruments to encode and decode information. It is not a bringing forth, in a Heideggerian sense; it is more of an exploiting: "The revealing that rules in modern technology is a challenging [*Herausfordern*], which puts to nature the unreasonable demand that it supply energy that can be extracted and stored as such."[29]

This is a very important distinction to understand. The "challenging" pointed out here is contingent upon not just the extraction of what Heidegger calls energy, but the storing of it. He uses the example of a windmill, which uses the energy from the wind to grind grain or move water, but does not *store* that energy for future use.[30] To contrast this example, Heidegger points to "a tract of land" that "is challenged into the putting out of coal and ore." In this case, the land is transformed, classified—"reveal[ing] itself as a coal-mining district, the soil as a mineral deposit. The field that the peasant formerly cultivated and set in order . . . appears differently than it did when to set in order still meant to take care of and to maintain."[31] In this case, a technological (instrumental) approach has "set-in-order" the land in such a way that it has been classified into a system of resources. An instrumental approach here looks at the land as a repository of resources that must be extracted, rather than as an organic site of cultivation where the peasant had to work in accordance with the natural agricultural processes of growth.

Heidegger maintains that in modern times, through technology, we attempt a setting-in-order of nature itself: "Agriculture is now the mechanized food industry. Air is now set upon to yield nitrogen, the earth to yield ore, ore to yield uranium, for example; uranium is set upon to yield atomic energy, which can be released either for destruction or peaceful use."[32] Although "Modern technology" for Heidegger is a kind of revealing, it is fundamentally different from the bringing forth that the silversmith or peasant enacts. Instead, we "challenge forth" by setting-in-order. This revealing has an almost obsessive quality:

> The energy concealed in nature is unlocked, what is unlocked is transformed, what is transformed is stored up, what is stored up is, in turn, distributed, and what is distributed is switched over anew. Unlocking, transforming, storing, distributing, and switching about are ways of revealing, but revealing never simply comes to an end. Neither does it run off into the indeterminate. The revealing reveals to itself its own manifoldly interlocking paths, through regulating their course.[33]

Even though Heidegger did not have the immediate advantage of cybernetic theories of information at his disposal, it is not too much of a stretch to substitute "information" for "energy" in the example above. The model still holds. In fact, as Heidegger progresses, it becomes apparent that what exactly is "revealed" by this instrumental view of technology is actually information. "That which comes to stand forth" is the product of this process of uncovering, and in such a way the world is transformed:

> Everywhere everything is ordered to stand by, to be immediately at hand, indeed to stand there just so that it may be on call for a further ordering. Whatever is ordered about in this way has its own standing. We call it the standing-reserve [*Bestand*]. The word expresses here something more, and something more essential, than mere "stock."[34]

As we have already witnessed, in the posthuman view, all things can be broken down into code. It is not difficult to see how transforming things into code places them in a position to be "on call" or manipulated for future use.

As vulnerable as nature is to being codified into "standing-reserve," Heidegger maintains that humanity's ability to transform nature is still limited. Even though "man drives technology forward" and "takes part in ordering as a way of revealing," ordering is *all we can do* as humans. We are still subject to the forces of nature. We cannot *create* the raw materials which we fashion into objects.[35] The silversmith did not elementally create the silver. There is, and will always be, a dependence on the physicality of nature as a necessity of the human condition. Nature—the world—can never completely be the subject of human control. Best illustrated by critic John Zuern, nature reveals itself to us "on its own terms." We cannot directly control the elemental formation of matter in nature, "we can only control the way we *orient* ourselves, our thinking and our actions, in relation to such resources."[36]

The instrumental view of technology, and the sciences which have been born through it, observes and investigates nature in a particular way, transforming it into "an object of research, until even the object disappears into the objectlessness of the standing-reserve."[37] What we consider to be "real" is transformed into a standing-reserve, much in the same way that posthumanism views the world as composed of information. For Heidegger, the manner in which we view and orient ourselves in the world is called *enframing*.[38]

It is important to remember that enframing *does not* imply an instrumental view of technology in and of itself. The process of enframing does not have to be enacted to privilege an instrumental point of view. Heidegger later tells us that we can orient ourselves in such a way that we are not hindered by instrumentality. However, instrumentality *is* the manner in which modern science (at least from Heidegger's perspective) orients itself in relation to nature. The *process* of enframing is not technological, but modern science enframes nature technologically. Thus, the "standing-reserve" in a contemporary scientific idiom *would be information*. Heidegger himself makes this maneuver possible when he states that "Modern science's way of representing pursues and entraps nature as a calculable coherence of forces. Modern physics . . . orders its experiments precisely for the purpose of asking whether and how nature reports itself when set up this way."[39]

For Heidegger, the cornerstone of modern physics is the fact that "nature reports itself in some way or other that it is identifiable through calculation and that it remains *orderable as a system of information*."[40] The world as standing-reserve—as information—not only becomes knowable, but it also promises us the possibility of controlling nature itself. Indeed, the *essence* of technology, for Heidegger, is not the artifacts or systems of technology, but the very *human* frame of mind through which we view the world. It is the "human drive for a precise, controllable knowledge of the natural world."[41] The very human act of enframing becomes the essence of technology.

Presenting the essence of technology as a human drive represents a missed opportunity for posthumanism. Whether we view posthumanism complacently as a replacement for humanism, or critically as a means to "work through" humanism in light of technology, both approaches privilege instrumental technology itself over the human, glossing over the actual moment of interface between them and how our need for technology manifests itself theoretically, psychologically, and ontologically. Not even Hayles at her most thoughtful and vigilant characterizes technology as a "natural" aspect of humanity. By placing too much emphasis on technology as "other," we have lost our own natural connections to it.

Enframing Nightmares, Enframing Dreams

Since enframing is a natural aspect of human consciousness (in that it is the way in which we apprehend the world) then, according to Heidegger, "the question as to how we are to relate to the essence of technology . . . always comes too late."[42] The best we can do is gain a different perspective on technology by investigating our own orientation to the world. It is important to remember, however, that enframing does not *automatically* put us in a state of transforming the world into information ("standing-reserve"). Within the process of enframing, there is the possibility "for a different—we might say 'renewed' orientation to the world."[43] If the essence of technology is actually our own orientation to the world, we could, possibly "open ourselves" to establish a different, more "free" relationship to technology.[44]

The underlying danger of technology, according to Heidegger, is not the threat "from the potentially lethal machines and apparatus of technology," but rather that "the rule of enframing threatens man with the possibility that it could be denied to him to enter into a more original revealing and hence experience the call of a more primal truth."[45] It is not technology itself which threatens us; it is the way in which we choose to engage technology. The fault does not lie with the technological systems we use, but the power, and faith, we invest in them. By becoming enmeshed—even obsessed—by the "frenziedness of ordering"[46] which modern technology makes possible, we could lose sight of the "truth."

This truth, which ultimately can be called Heidegger's own posthuman dream, reveals the responsibility that we have *to* the world to bring into being that which is good: which is, for Heidegger, art.[47] We must keep in mind here that the "art" Heidegger discusses here is not simply works of art (i.e., paintings, sculpture, architecture), but instead implies an object created as more than simply a means to an end. "Art" here is closer to an object created that addresses a specific need, more along the lines of Scarry's characterization of technological artifacts that are created as a way to express certain internal states. Thus, a simple tool such as a hammer can be a "work of art" in that it represents a means of expression and is a direct connection with the world teleologically.

Truth is a process of revealing. Through art, we can take part in the process of bringing something into being without being pressured into classifying or exploiting the resources of the world.[48] Technology becomes an aspect of knowing, not as a method to transform nature (datafying it) into something we can use, but instead as a way of revealing the possibilities and intricacies of nature and the world—and recognizing our own *responsibility* to nature as the agents by which nature is revealed.

There are similarities here to posthumanism, especially in the attempt to make the human being more relevant in the technological world, but what Heidegger articulates is actually something which contemporary posthumanism *implies*, but seems too preoccupied to state directly: that technology is an aspect of human epistemology. Heidegger's starting point—that technology is actually a human way of knowing—is actually closer to posthumanism's *conclusion*. Posthuman dreams embrace technology in order to extend the scope of human awareness. They are predicated on the idea that technology is a *separate entity that can be embraced in order to achieve a new kind of epistemology*, rather than the idea that technology—its essence—was and is based on the manner in which humans enframe the world. Heidegger implicates technology as the foundation and mechanism behind human awareness itself.

Strategically separating the "instrumental" from the "essence" of technology, Heidegger has anticipated the gaps in the cyborg and the posthuman by emphasizing the human drive which gives birth to technology. He also articulated the obsessive revealing and "complexification" which posthumanism—even critical posthumanism—actually fosters through its assumption that the degree of our humanity is proportional to the degree of our compatibility with information.

In posthumanism, the extending of awareness is dependent upon technological systems: we cannot achieve a "posthuman dream" without the technology which supplements us. The more complex the system, the greater the potential for human "transcendence." Paradoxically, the greater the potential for human "transcendence," the greater the possibility that the human will be lost. For Heidegger, technology has always been a "part" of us. It has been, and seemingly always will be, what makes humanism possible. The goal of technology is not to further the human; instead, it should reveal how much we actually *matter* in the world. There is a slight—but important—difference between Heidegger's emphasis on humans mattering in the world and Hayles's desire to reach "full embodied awareness." The former more distinctly implicates us as participants in the world, while the latter remains more true to a humanist prerogative of emphasizing human subjectivity as differentiated from the world itself. Posthumanism here actually furthers the self/other paradigm which it seeks to "work through."

What Heidegger offers us is a more realistic approach to understanding the possibilities of a posthumanist subjectivity. By characterizing technology as *both* a means of expression *and* a means of apprehending the world, he maintains a balance between the instrumental and epistemological that posthumanism finds difficult to achieve. That is not to say that we should limit ourselves to a Heideggerian approach. Instead, we should look to Heidegger as a first step toward understanding the articulation of posthuman subjectivity. For the human relationship to technology is, especially now, more complex than even Heidegger could foresee. Even though his "standing reserve" can be equated with contemporary concepts of information, we cannot ignore the significance we attribute to information, and how, in more contemporary terms, we attempt to deal with information that has been revealed.

Lyotard's *Inhuman*:
Information and Posthuman Reality

If technology is a part of how we enframe the world, then how and why has information risen to such stature that it could be given the same status as material instantiation? How does the use of technology "prime" us to privilege information in such a manner, and serve to alienate us from our technological artifacts and what we perceive as the data which constitutes us? It is here that we turn to Jean François Lyotard's *The Inhuman* to understand how a human need for information rearticulates itself into a need for instrumental technology.

Lyotard translates Heidegger's basic concepts of information and the human's relationship to the standing reserve into more contemporary terms, and also takes an unapologetic approach to exactly how dependent on technology human beings actually are. Through a further qualification of what defines the technological and what defines the human, Lyotard re-centers our humanity in our ability to recognize ourselves and situate that recognition via narrative. He maintains that narrative is the uniquely human means by which we self-reflexively sort, remember, and interpret information.

Lyotard offers us a further clarification of the human limitations which eventually stand at the heart of posthumanist discourse. His characterization of human suffering as a recognition of the "inexhaustibility of the perceivable" complements Scarry's theories of human expression, and helps identify the motives behind posthumanism's desire to transcend technology through technology.

In the *Inhuman*, Lyotard discusses many of the issues which posthumanism addresses, but pays special attention to what can only be called the "realities" of our relationship with technology, as well as the realities of our own human evolution. What sets Lyotard apart from others we have discussed so far, however, is his almost immediate acknowledgment of humanity's utter reliance upon technology. Pointing out that the sun has only 4.5 billion years left before it collapses, Lyotard tells us that the survival of all human endeavor, including philosophy itself, is contingent upon our ability either to leave the planet as a species and thus forgo the "natural" relationship we have with the earth, or create a way to retain human subjectivity in a non-human, perhaps non-biological substrate.[49] The obliteration of the earth would preclude any and all *human* activity, including the possibility of witnessing our own extinction. In order for thought to survive, we must, as a species, be willing to give up a traditionally defined, earth-bound humanity. This is the reality of the human condition, according to Lyotard.

This acknowledgment of the "end" of humanity here differs from what we see in posthumanist discourse, mainly because it is not an end that humanity brings upon itself. Rather than claim responsibility for the possible "conclusion" of humanity as a species (whether it's a critical transcendence or a complacent abandonment), Lyotard strategically repositions subjectivity in the equation. This is the first in a series of human "relocations" that Lyotard enacts in order to re-situate humanity in a much larger scheme. Rather than attacking the validity of the humanist subject, or romanticizing humanity's ability to bring things into being, Lyotard de-centers the human in order to achieve a needed perspective.

As human beings, we see ourselves as responsible for technological progress. But—in what becomes Lyotard's most provocative claim—technology is *not* a unique human endeavor: "You know—technology wasn't invented by us humans."[50] He maintains that even the smallest life forms can be viewed as information processing "devices":

> Any material system is technological if it filters information useful to its survival, if it memorizes and processes that information and makes inferences based on the regulating effect of behaviour, that is, if it intervenes on and impacts its environment so as to assure its perpetuation at least. A human being isn't different in nature from an object of this type.[51]

In a slight, but highly significant departure from Heidegger, Lyotard not only places technology as an inescapable aspect of humanity, but goes even further by stating that technology (defined as the ability to process and manipulate information) is a characteristic of biological life itself and *is not* uniquely human. Lyotard's "relocation" of the human begins.

What does make us unique as human beings, however, is our ability to think and to "take into account" our own ability to process data: in other words, our ability to be aware of ourselves.[52] Humans are technological beings like any other living organism, but technological beings *who recognize themselves as such*. Lyotard shows us that this recognition announces itself through language, and that narrative is the primary means by which humans process, store, and give meaning to information. Narrative is the way in which we process the information—whether that information is revealed instrumentally (through scientific/technological systems), or if it is taken in directly by our senses. Narrative is our own uniquely human way of making sense of things. Like Heidegger, Lyotard provides us with a strategic approach toward technology which distinguishes between the more instrumental aspects of technology (its artifacts and systems) from what is essentially a human way of coming to know the world.

Posthumanism, by contrast, never adequately attempts to distinguish between technology's instrumentality and what humans actually use technology for, or what we actually expect from it. Posthumanist subjectivity is presented as the ongoing human attempt to distinguish ourselves from the technological other. The erosion of human agency is viewed as a symptom of an uninformed world-view which does not take into account, or fully appreciate, the boundaries between the human and the technological.

Paradoxically, the only way to be aware of those boundaries is through the very technological systems which cause our ignorance in the first place. Post-humanist discourse attempts to re-define subjectivity in response to the presence of the technological other. But it does not take into account that the subject has always used technology to define itself. By contrast, Lyotard implies that the recognition of the self can actually be characterized as a technological process.

For Lyotard, and to some extent Heidegger as well, "humanism" and "post-humanism" would essentially be the same thing, since technology and humanity, epistemologically speaking, are inseparable. But, as with Heidegger and the posthumanists, there is always some kind of "fissure" that opens where humanity and technology attempt to come together. Ironically, the wider the fissure, the more blind we are to it. When technology's instrumentality seems the most ubiquitous, when our relationship to it seems the closest, technology has the potential to make us "forget" ourselves. As the technological systems and artifacts we use become most effective, our self-image is extended through our expanded ability to affect change on the world around us.

Posthumanism's reliance upon the privileging of "informational pattern over material instantiation"[53] becomes highly significant here, because if information is considered *more important* than material instantiation (via the belief that all things—humans included—are composed of physical expressions of coded data), the ability to manipulate information itself is privileged. According to Lyotard, as we become more technologically advanced, we tend to place more value on the simple act of "uncovering" or "unlocking" information than we do on understanding the significance of that information. "All technology . . . is an artefact [*sic*] allowing its users to stock more information, to improve their competence and optimize their performances."[54] This has the effect of leading us to equate the human efficacy not with true understanding (in a Heideggerian sense), but with the ability to uncover and store information. Granted, we do so with the hope of some day being able to *manipulate* that information—but to what ends? Most often, only to uncover and unlock *more information*; information which we, as humans, can apprehend only with the aid of even more advanced technological instruments and systems.

The more information we can uncover, the more deeply implicated in technological systems we become; we become more dependent on technology's instrumentality to "challenge forth" that information. In this model, human efficacy becomes dependent—and often challenged by—our ability to maintain control over our technological systems. The human race, in Lyotard's words, must "rise to the new complexity" and "dehumanize itself."[55] To "rise to the new complexity" is to find the means to make the self fully translatable and transferable to the machine. What Lyotard identifies here is basically what post-humanism is attempting to do—rise to complexity and make the human more compatible with technological systems. Although critical posthumanism is trying to do so with the best interests of humanity in mind, it is still doing so in a way that actually furthers the idea that consciousness is merely an informational pattern, and is susceptible to technological means of inscription and reinscription.

Lyotard does address the possibility of uploading the consciousness to a machine, but points out that first the machine must be advanced enough to support the complexity of thought itself. Any machine-based body designed to "house" the mind must be capable of supporting the reflexivity of human cognition—the ability for the subject to recognize itself.[56] Ultimately, however, Lyotard maintains that such an uploading is predicated upon the belief that cognition *is separable* from the human body. In contemporary terms, the physical body becomes hardware, and thought becomes software.

The main problem with this kind of mind uploading model is the same problem that critical posthumanists have pointed out: it is contingent upon a reinscription of the humanist subject (something Lyotard acknowledges). But Lyotard does not stop there. Paul Harris explains that "the brain has become a privileged site to locate and anchor the human," and it functions to ground the subject—especially in light of how the subject is decentered in postmodern philosophy. However, in order to be the "locus of subjectivity, the brain has had to emerge as an empirical object."[57] The brain becomes a component in a body whose role has been de-emphasized:

> From Lyotard's viewpoint, the brain serves as a kind of interface where the evolutionary "human" situates itself at the apex of technoscientific "development" and "complexification." Simultaneously, though, the technoscientific development or "progress" that extends our knowledge of the brain expropriates it from its privileged place. For once the "human" is located in the brain, and the brain can be understood scientifically and perhaps technologically, then the brain becomes a site that enables a different "human" to emerge.[58]

This model applies to critical posthumanism as well, especially when we consider the repeated calls for humans to embrace technology in order that a "more human" human being emerge. For Lyotard, the "human" that emerges is not human at all, but is instead simply an agent of a more cosmological process of "complexification."

Development:
The Ultimate Posthuman Nightmare

The posthuman nightmare does not go unnoticed in Lyotard, who sees "uncontested humanism"[59] much in the same manner as Badmington sees complacent posthumanism. For Lyotard, this uncontested humanism is "becoming incorporated into a 'system' whose motive drive is that of 'development' . . . the system's ontology is one of 'information'; its developmental logic is that of 'complexification.'"[60] Complexification is a slippery concept in Lyotard, for he never truly explicates its meaning other than by associating it with "development" or "negative entropy." Generally speaking, complexification stands against the natural tendency for any given system to come to rest. Lyotard's usage links the term to information: any system undergoing complexification is experiencing an influx of information and *actively attempting to adapt to that information* so that it may be used to further the development of that system.[61]

If we take into account the idea that technology is a "fact of life" (all life, not just human life), then the development and evolution of any given species can be attributed to its complexification—its increased ability to handle information more effectively. Taking this line of reasoning to its ultimate conclusion, Lyotard sees human "techno-scientific development" as "the present-day form of a process of negentropy or complexification that has been underway since the earth began its existence . . . human beings aren't and never have been the motor of this complexification, but an effect and carrier of this negentropy, its continuer."[62] Humans themselves become the instruments of complexification, rather than the other way around.

Humbled, the human race suffers "another blow to . . . human narcissism."[63] Citing Freud, Lyotard tells us that not only are we no longer the "centre of the cosmos (Copernicus) . . . the first living creature (Darwin) . . . [or] the master of meaning," but we are not responsible for our own development—neither biological *nor* technological. We do not have "the monopoly of mind, that is, Complexification."[64] Instead, we are "a transformer, ensuring, through technoscience, arts, economic development, cultures . . . a supplement of complexity in the universe."[65] Again, Lyotard's language here calls to mind Heidegger's implication that the human being acts as an agent of transformation, re-classifying nature into a series of "natural *resources*" to be exploited. Yet Lyotard takes this one step further by placing this drive to transform in the cosmological realm, and dislodging technology as being unique to humans, characterizing it as a aspect of all living beings.

Along the same lines, technological progress necessarily *does not* have the best interest of the present human species in mind. Remember, Lyotard reiterates that "the essential objectives of research today" are to overcome human physical limitations—"the obstacles the body places in the way of development."[66] Superficially, this may seem to be something that is most definitely in our best interest (especially if we are to escape the death of the sun). But development is instead "making the body adaptable to non-terrestrial conditions of life, or of substituting another 'body' for it."[67] Lyotard implies that achieving this "non-terrestrial condition" is predicated on what is the end of the human biological species *as we know it*. Lyotard does *not* go as far as to say that development will bring about some kind of "transcendence," but he does—albeit surreptitiously—imply that development does assume the end of *homo sapiens*.[68]

What Lyotard does here is take an unflinchingly realistic view of the human condition, but he does so from an larger, cosmological standpoint. In some respects, we could use this as a "calling out" of critical posthumanism. As Hayles' posthuman and Haraway's cyborg make ready for our fully realized potential,

Lyotard asks (and answers) the question "to what end?" That is, on the most basic level, the question that critical posthumanism has the most difficulty coming to terms with: to what "end" do we use technology?

Of course, the more obvious critical posthuman answer would be "to achieve full embodied awareness." But this answer comes too quickly, too easily, and without first looking at the most fundamental level at which the human engages technology: we use technology to get things done. Technological artifacts extend our reach, enhancing our ability to affect the world around us, in order that we may achieve tasks that are impossible without technology.

Ironically, the question "to what end?" answers itself. In terms of instrumentality, we use technology primarily as a means to achieve an "end." It allows us to "complete" tasks—to engage in a task until there is no longer any need for the task itself. Temporally speaking, we may say that we've "finished it" or that the task is "done," but what we have actually done is "filled up" or saturated it. Although the task might need to be repeated later, at the moment we engage it, there is a set point where the task can no longer be performed to bring about a change (e.g., the lawn needs mowing. Once it is cut to the desired height, it cannot be mowed any more).

The problem arises when we equate technologically inspired concepts of completion with our own more narrative (and temporal) human instincts for conclusion: the task is completed and *thus I may now move on*. Or we "complete" a task conditionally where the completion of a given task signals the beginning of others ("I need to finish the lawn before I can fix the storm window"). We tend to mark our progress by the list of completed tasks we have achieved, or, more often, we view the tasks that need completing as conditions for conclusion itself ("I cannot bring my day to a close until I have completed x, y, and z"). Such tasks become marks of our progress. Our faith in technology comes with an often implicit codicil: that our progress—our moving forward—is dependent on our technology. But, as Lyotard points out, progress does not necessarily bring with it insight or knowledge.

This is where we see Lyotard at his most prescient. For the human species in our present—posthuman—state, "progress" often has an alienating effect. Even though we are uncovering more and more information at an exponential rate, Lyotard tells us that "the penetration of techno-scientific apparatus into the cultural field in no way signifies an increase of knowledge, sensibility, tolerance, and liberty. . . . Experience shows rather the reverse: a new barbarism, illiteracy and impoverishment of language, new poverty . . . immiseration of the mind, [and] obsolescence of the soul."[69] Similar to Scarry's approach in *The Body in Pain*, Lyotard notes a certain loss of human skill as our machines become more complex. As technology advances, we paradoxically become *more* ignorant, and, as a species, become even more removed from development. Complexification reigns. "The human race is . . . 'pulled forward' by this process without possessing the slightest capacity for mastering it. It has to adapt to the new conditions."[70]

This new barbarism is exactly what critical posthumanism fears. But by implying that achieving our true human potential is dependent on the quality of our relationship with technology, posthumanism helps to make such barbarism possible. Critical posthumanism implies that all the information we need is available, so long as we have the right apparatus by which to understand it. The power we invest in our technological systems is similar to the same powers our more primitive ancestors invested in their own fetishes. What power do we expect from the cell phones in our pockets, or the computer terminals to which we conform our bodies?

The answer becomes apparent only when we look at our instinctive reactions when those artifacts fail us. When our technology fails, it is most often characterized as a loss that impedes our progress: a lost signal, lost data, lost connections, lost productivity, etc. When the dreaded "no signal" message flashes across or cell phone displays, we almost instinctively look up. What are we looking for? We shake the phone—perhaps even hit it. And then we hold it up toward the sky, hoping to "receive" (or perhaps, *be granted*) a signal. And when our computers "freeze," or stop working, we attempt more physical—even primitive—interfaces with it. We start hitting it, begging it, even holding either side of the monitor with our hands as if we were addressing a misbehaving child. Or, in the most extreme cases, we treat it as a dying loved one. "Please . . . please don't do this. Please come back to me. I need you."

At those moments, it may seem superficially that we are suffering because our tools are not allowing us to complete a given task and hindering our progress. However, we are actually suffering because our technological artifacts are not *acknowledging us*. They are not perceiving the "pain" of our incomplete human condition. They are not responding to us the way we need them to. We are rendered insignificant in the face of a technological system which we believe, we hope, we wish to be superior.

Lyotard performs a kind of posthuman-backhand—giving technological development a cosmological significance, but then de-emphasizing humanity by characterizing us as simply agents, not purveyors, of technological development. For Lyotard, as we seem to "move forward" in our system of technological development, we actually become more "discontent":

> The system . . . has the consequence of causing the forgetting of what escapes it. But the anguish is that of a mind haunted by a familiar and unknown guest which is agitating it, sending it delirious but also making it think—if one claims to exclude it, if one doesn't give it an outlet, one aggravates it. Discontent grows with this civilization, foreclosure along with information.[71]

It is not technological development in and of itself which causes "anguish," but instead the human ability to recognize development, and the meaning we do or do not associate with that recognition. We hold ourselves up to a model of development, looking toward technological systems as examples of how to achieve our own individual "progress." Lyotard identifies what I will call a "posthuman condition" that characterizes humanity as the agent of complexification, whose role in development is characterized as an almost compulsive desire to uncover and manipulate information, making us believe that our development and efficacy is predicated on this uncovering of information.

The anguish, or suffering, that Lyotard points out here is similar to the suffering Scarry outlines, in that both represent different aspects of our human failure to express ourselves. For Scarry, suffering comes from an inability to share one's pain, which in turn causes doubt in the person who witnesses that pain: the human suffers from an inability to express perception. Lyotard's anguish resides at the other side of the equation, so to speak, where the human must shoulder the burden of knowing that there is always more to be known. Paradoxically, both cause the human to turn to technology as a means to ease that suffering and anguish. For Lyotard, suffering does not arise as a result of development per se, but instead comes from the human *recognition* of development as an entity outside of ourselves, and the consequent need to "catch up" with what seems to be constantly surpassing us.

This catching up is a manifestation of the enigmatic "profound injury" which Haraway speaks of in her "Cyborg Manifesto." At some point, humans have been separated from a more natural relationship with technology. The utter speed at which information is made available has surpassed our ability to process that information. We must endeavor to purposefully use that information, rather than to reveal or uncover it obsessively.

Although complexification is a fact of life and necessary for the survival of humanity (or some *aspect* of humanity), Lyotard does offer a kind of alternative to the blind staggering forward of progress. He proposes a "different mode of thinking" as an alternative, or more correctly, *an alterity*, in relation to complexification: the Freudian process of *anamnesis*. In this context, anamnesis is a kind of "beginning again, in order to slow down, go back, gather the frayed threads of thoughts forgotten by the frantic push of the system's development."[72] Similar to posthumanist critics, Lyotard maintains that it is only through thoughtful examination that we can be aware of our relationship with technology. But unlike posthumanist critics, Lyotard proposes an actual method by which this can be achieved.

Complexification and the Suffering (Post)Human

Before we can investigate the process of anamnesis, we must pause for a moment to resituate ourselves in light of Lyotard's claim that technology is *not* uniquely human. This, of course, takes away what is so often cited as one of the defining characteristics of the human race. Taking technology out of the equation, we are thus left with subjectivity as our claim to developmental uniqueness. We return to Lyotard's idea that the true mark of the human is self awareness—

the ability to take into account our own ability to process information. Most importantly, however, this self-awareness manifests itself as narrative.

This reinscription of the humanist subject is nothing new in regard to the theorists we have already encountered. However, what sets Lyotard apart is his claim that human subjectivity is narrative in nature, and that narrative is the way that human beings take in and order the information that constitutes experience. At best, posthumanists rely solely on the idea of *cognition* as the defining human trait, and while each makes valiant attempts at deconstructing the liberal humanist subject, they do so by the *addition* of technology, and treating it as a supplement to cognition, rather than—in Heidegger and Lyotard's case—making cognition contingent upon technology.

By subsuming technology as part of the human condition (indeed, as part of being itself), Lyotard centers our human-ness in a different area. And it is this aspect of humanity which Lyotard feels *cannot* be replicated by a machine. This aspect is grounded in our human limitations. As humans, our ability to perceive the world is limited. These limits "are always beyond reach."[73] Using vision as a model, Lyotard explains: "While a visual object is presenting one side to the eye, there are always other sides, still unseen. A direct, focused vision is always surrounded by a curved area where visibility is held in reserve yet isn't absent."[74] When we look at an object from a different angle, we are always "preserv[ing] along with it what was seen an instant before from another angle. It anticipates what will be seen shortly."[75] Thus, when we process the visual input we receive, we are able to identify the objects we are looking at—but not completely. Another sighting of the object can "unsettle or undo" the identification we made previously.

According to Lyotard, the eye "is indeed always in search of a recognition, as the mind is of a complete description of an object it is trying to think of."[76] We can never "recognize an object perfectly" because "the field of presentation is unique every time . . . there is always more to be seen once the object is 'identified.' Perceptual 'recognition' never satisfies the logical demand for complete description."[77] It is this belief that there is always something more to be known, this "faith in the inexhaustibility of the perceivable,"[78] which is part of the uniquely human condition. Like a writer who has an almost infinite combination of words at his or her disposal, the biological human is faced with the knowledge that the majority of what is to be both taken in and expressed will always remain hidden. The "suffering" that arises from this limitation is—for Lyotard—an inescapable aspect of human experience.

Lyotard tells us that "thinking and suffering overlap."[79] When we attempt to express ourselves, the means of expression (whether it is through writing, art, music, dance, etc.), always hold within themselves vast "possibilities of meaning."[80] Echoing Heidegger, Lyotard characterizes thinking as "almost no more than letting a giveable come towards you."[81] In other words, we are apprehending what the world has to give us. Again, we are reminded of Scarry's contention that technological artifacts are a means to make us "more available" to the world.[82]

However, Lyotard adds another dimension to this suffering which Scarry does not: this process of thinking is also rooted in *time*. We have a duty to express what *must* be signified: "Maybe that duty isn't a debt. Maybe it's just the mode according to which what doesn't yet exist, a word, a phrase, a colour, *will emerge*. So that the suffering of thinking is a suffering of time, of what happens."[83]

Suffering is the means by which we are rooted in time *and* space. As Harris points out, "the key turn in Lyotard's account of thought is that this suffering must be transposed from an incompleteness of an end, the play of unrealizable potentialities, to the opening at a beginning."[84] The temporality of suffering allows us to recognize the opportunity for expression. In the most basic terms, we have a limited time to express our thoughts and thus achieve our goals. Lyotard himself points out the ultimate time constraint as the death of the sun. To exacerbate this condition, our own ability to remember is fragile. As time progresses, it becomes increasingly difficult to hold onto the experiences and information we have "stored." Our narratives themselves are fragile.

For Lyotard, a machine lacks the ability to express itself because its defining code is too static. Because of its ability to store everything it senses and have it available at all times, it cannot "suffer" in the same way we do. A machine cannot experience the angst connected with the "inexhaustibility of the perceivable," because there is no fragility of memory to frame what could be remembered. It is this aspect of "faith" which distinguishes the suffering *human* from the more inhuman "drive" toward development. What makes us human in Lyotard's view is our ability to "break" from the compulsive, techno-scientific drive to uncover information and use the information that we have uncovered as a means to create an "opening" which makes our "receiving of the world" possible. In other words, a defining characteristic of our humanity is our narrative ability to pause and attempt a more conscious, recursive, and thoughtful interpretation of the information which we perceive. This is how we are to perform a process of "working through" the information complexification has revealed.

Anamnesis:
The Narrative Alternative to Complexification

In strictly Freudian terms, anamnesis is a "working through" of past traumatic events. More than a simple remembering, it is a kind of critical re-experiencing of past events in such a way that the patient is able to maintain a more cohesive, centralized point of view from which to interpret the experiences which initially had been forgotten. For Lyotard, complexification's relentless progress pulls us forward without giving us a chance to understand what is occurring. Furthermore, our human desire to "recognize an object perfectly" and our "faith in the inexhaustibility of the perceivable" only exacerbate our posthuman condition of being pulled forward by complexification: we believe the only means by which

we can attempt to know what is perceivable is through more advanced technological systems. Thus, the process of complexification pulls us forward even more
quickly.

Lyotard is most reliant on the idea of anamnesis not as a "dialectical move
toward synthesis, but rather an internal *displacement*—spatial and temporal—
against a system of meanings."[85] In order to work through the information that
complexification reveals to us, we must be mindful of the past, and "freely asso-
ciat[e] incompatible elements with past situations"[86] lest the trauma repeat itself.
But what, in the process of complexification, presents itself as trauma? For Lyotard, it is "what could not have been forgotten because it was never inscribed."[87]
In keeping with the model of the human being as a "transformer," where information is extracted and held, there is no time for *meaning* to be brought forth.
We can obsessively decode (and even encode) but never truly translate or interpret. We are haunted by experiences we do not understand, yet driven to progress
forward. The initial event of experience "functions as something like a trauma,
something that escapes representation and therefore inscription."[88]

Similar to the analysand in Freud, we are plagued by gaps in "memory" for
which we cannot account. As Harris explains, "Lyotard's anamnesis represents a
generalization of this model as a dynamic of thought where the mind works back
through the lost shards of past situations and reintegrates them in a process that
gives thinking the space and time to emerge."[89] Lyotard articulates something
which Heidegger seemingly could not—the difference between a "frenzied ordering" of the world, and the opportunity which technology gives us to arrive at
"truth." By relying on the process of anamnesis as a "threading together of disparate and discarded materials,"[90] Lyotard sets up *narrative* as the means by
which we can more mindfully situate ourselves in light of complexification.
Narratives also serve as an alternative to the instant "memorization" which
modern technology puts at our disposal.

The posthuman does not take this more narrative aspect of our humanity into account. Although it does use terms such as "coding" and "inscription," these
are technologically-inspired metaphors that imply a kind of storing or memorization of information. How we meaningfully *interpret* the information at our
disposal—or the "significance" of the technology we attempt to use—is never
taken into account. Even though we now have more advanced and complex
means for storing information, humans still "make sense" of information narratively. Lyotard points out that "the narrative . . . can be considered to be a technical apparatus giving a people the means to store, order, and retrieve units of
information, i.e. events. More precisely, narratives are like temporal filters
whose function is to transform the emotive charge linked to the event into se-
quences of units of information capable of giving rise to something like meaning."[91] If all living beings are technological in that they process information,
what makes human beings unique in light of technological development is the
narrative, self-reflexive way in which we assign meaning to information.

The posthuman condition is plagued by complexification. We are pulled
forward by technological progress and our very human faith in the inexhaustibil-

ity of the perceivable—the belief that there is always more information to un-cover, to store, and eventually understand. Anamnesis is not simply a way to *interpret* that information; it is a way to reposition ourselves in relation to that information. Lyotard implies that it is a way to achieve a certain vantage point which relies upon our very human quality of narration to make more *meaningful* connections with the information that instrumental technology has made availa-ble to us. Anamnesis is a process of re-establishing us as a participant in a more technologically-defined world, rather than as a marginalized spectator, merely witnessing ourselves being "re-coded" and "re-defined" according to technolo-gical models of efficiency and completion.

This is something that does not go unnoticed in critical posthumanism. Both Katherine Hayles and Donna Haraway call for a "re-positioning" of the human in relation to the technological other which is similar to anamnesis in its "step-ping back" and reclaiming of a certain authority of inscription. However, the critical posthumanist interpretation of anamnesis characterizes the process in a slightly different manner—but with very significant results. Returning to Bad-mington's "Theorizing Posthumanism," we see a recognition of anamnesis not only as a possible means to "work through" the humanism inherent in posthu-manism, but also *as a means to an end*. He believes that

> the writing of the posthumanist condition should . . . take the form of a critical practice that occurs *inside* humanism, consisting not of the wake but the work-ing-through of humanist discourse. . . . A working through remains underway, and this coming to terms is, of course, a gradual and difficult process that lacks sudden breaks. An uneasy patience is called for . . . I think that questioning humanism—posthumanism itself—begins to build ways for being different in the future.[92]

The critical posthumanism that Badmington calls for is a logical continuation of Hayles's and Haraway's work—and is more clearly a kind of anamnesis. How-ever, it is one that lacks a recognition or understanding of the pre-existing, onto-logical and epistemological link between humanity and technology which Lyo-tard and Heidegger identify. It calls for a coming to terms without defining the terms in the first place. Although, for Badmington, anamnesis represents a way to work through humanism, the humanism he identifies is actually a product of complexification itself. It is a view of human subjectivity influenced by the exis-tence of the technological other. While the alternative of anamnesis is attractive to critical posthumanists in that it allows for a more deliberate approach regard-ing the relationship between the human and technology, a posthumanist applica-tion characterizes anamnesis as a task to be completed, rather than as an ongoing process and characteristic of humanity.

Anamnesis relies on narrative: it requires us to re-integrate certain events, memories, and experiences into our frame of reference. In Lyotard's model— even though he presents anamnesis as an "alternative" to complexification—it is still something that is enacted *in response* to complexification. Lyotard re-

positions technology as the information-processing characteristic of all biological life. He then re-positions humanity (human subjectivity) as a self-reflexive
recognition of our own information processing. Thus, the *meaning* we attribute
to information always comes *after the fact*. Posthumanism, however, centers
human subjectivity in the act of complexification itself. "Recognition" and the
significance we attribute to information are not addressed.

The "blind staggering forward" Lyotard characterizes is an apt metaphor for
the posthumanist discourse. If we are staggering forward blindly, then we are
not really *looking* for anything. The blind man does not stagger forward to see;
he staggers forward to *feel*. He searches for something to hold onto, something
to help him define the space around him. And if he is staggering *forward*, then
he is doing so with a certain direction in mind, and a desire to make progress
toward a specific goal—but one he isn't able to see. Posthumanism is, in every
respect of the phrase, still grasping for some*thing*.

Strictly speaking, anamnesis, as a process, relies on a certain *stillness*, implying that the it can only make sense of *what has already occurred*, not what is
occurring in the present moment. Anamnesis is a *process of integration*, not a
goal to be achieved in and of itself. If we were to characterize it as a goal, then it
is subsumed into the very act of "staggering forward." Badmington sets up
anamnesis as a step, or component, toward reaching the goal of critical posthumanism—*achieving an understanding* that will eventually lead us to transcendence. True anamnesis, however, (especially as presented by Lyotard) maintains
that technology is a way to make the ongoing process of "working though" possible, but not for any specific end.

There is a vast difference in these two characterizations. Badmington's
posthumanist interpretation places anamnesis as a means to achieve an end—a
step in the process of moving forward. Lyotard presents anamnesis as simply an
ongoing process *made possible by* technological complexification. There is no
"end-point" to anamnesis: it is an ongoing process which we may (or may not)
engage in as a means to make sense of past events. In fact, Lyotard himself was
skeptical of the "use" of anamnesis as a means to achieve any specific goal.[93]

Furthermore, anamnesis needs a coherent point of view so that the individual can differentiate and re-situate him or herself against the background of
events and experience themselves. Once again, subjectivity is indirectly privileged. Also, in the strictest Freudian terms, anamnesis requires *the supplement*
of the analyst in order for it to be successful. The traumatized individual cannot
achieve this process alone. Thus, anamnesis requires not only a cohesive subject,
but also a supplement (or other) to allow the process to occur. Thus the process
relies on the same liberal humanist constructs (a supplement, a cohesive self,
and a privileging of technological metaphor) which posthumanism wants to
avoid.

Of course, engaging the system from within—using the discourse of the
system itself to deconstruct the system—is the defining characteristic of anamnesis. But in a strictly Freudian sense, one must still acknowledge the limitations
of the relationship with the supplemental "other" that is making the process

possible. Posthumanism has yet to acknowledge these limitations. It is also interesting to note that Badmington himself does not attempt to find out why a *psychoanalytic* process stands as a possible methodology to understand posthuman subjectivity, especially considering the fact that anamnesis is an avowedly narrative approach.

This is where examining the more Freudian foundations of posthumanism will be beneficial. It may be too strong of a statement to say that Freud was the first posthumanist, but he was among the first to perform a posthuman maneuver of holding the human up to a technological metaphor. Freud also seemed to be haunted by the same limitations found in critical posthumanism—especially in regard to the "ends" each seeks to achieve. Both posthumanism and psychoanalysis hold the human up to technological models of balance and order, and both attempt *narrative means* to engage those models. Both suffer because of it.

Freudian Psychoanalysis:
Posthumanism's Hidden Influence

Critical posthumanism relies on a psychoanalytic process to "come to terms with itself." If we look at the core assumptions of posthumanism—and its overall privileging of technological systems—we will see a very Freudian influence. More importantly, by investigating this influence, we can better understand the basic limitations of posthumanism. Posthumanism does not have the same goal as psychoanalysis; it is not (yet) an approach to dealing with various psychological difficulties. However, by taking a closer look at psychoanalytic theory, we can see that many of the assumptions Freud made regarding the nature of experience (characterizing it as information), the power of trauma and repression (information can have a direct *physical* influence on the body), and the centrality of human subjectivity (as a processor of information lacking *control* over information's interpretation), have a distinct correlation to posthumanism, and made many of posthumanism's core assumptions possible.

That is not to say that psychoanalysis was a *direct* influence on posthumanism, but I do believe it's fair to say that posthumanism would not be possible without psychoanalytic theory's early characterization of experience as a kind of information that had quantitative psychosomatic effects. Furthermore, the overall privileging of the thermodynamic model of balance as something to which a human could aspire also serves as an early precedent for the goals of cyborg "ethereality" and posthuman transcendence that surfaced over a century after the rise of psychoanalytic theory.

Posthumanism's submerged psychoanalytic influences tend to surface when theorists such as Hayles and Badmington call for various techniques of "working through" the complexities of posthuman subjectivity. Like Freud, each sees a need to situate subjectivity as a locus of control, re-establishing some kind of point of view in light of an originary "trauma." Unfortunately, the Freudian influence still remains buried enough that the limitations of analysis that Freud himself recognized still remain hidden in contemporary posthumanism. These limitations have a direct bearing on posthumanism's own ongoing attempts to "come to terms" with itself, as well as its desire to assist humans in coming to terms with technology.

Freud and Information

Freud's entire reconceptualization of the mind privileged technological concepts—specifically the metaphors of mechanisms and systems—as models. His approaches linked an understanding of the human (or, more importantly, the manner in which humans interpret their environment) with a more technological/scientific idea of balance and order. His underlying concept of the "ideal" mental state is comparable to that of a balanced thermodynamic system. Thus, the ideal human state is based upon a systematized model that is bound by technological metaphors and expectations of balance. The human-as-system is simply that, yet the human system *narratively* seeks balance via its ability to represent itself within a viable, self-generated pattern of existence.

One of Freud's final essays, "Analysis Terminable and Interminable," is marked by a discord between theoretical and practical applications of psychoanalytic theory, manifested as what best can be described as a conflict between the narrative approaches of psychoanalysis toward "cure" and Freud's higher aspirations toward what is actually a humanly impossible thermodynamic ideal of balance. His psychoanalytic theory is one of the first places where the conflict between narrative conclusion and technological completion becomes apparent. To be "cured" in a practical sense was marked by a conclusion of analysis, where the patient was "balanced enough" to function. In theoretical/scientific terms, being cured meant a complete—and humanly impossible—saturation of analysis, where all repression was lifted and no new traumas would take place.

Freud's use of technological metaphors wasn't simply a choice dictated by his specific scientific idiom, but was also indicative of a privileging of technology in general. His work is also marked by a conflict between the narrative interpretation of human experience needed in the psychoanalytic process, and his desire to validate such experience via a scientific/empirical approach.

The movement became entangled in itself very quickly: his theories attempt to fall back onto technologically informed metaphors and systems to *scientifically* engage human desire and experience in narrative terms, endowing the human narrative with the same type of power/resonance that posthumanism places in information. Subjectivity then becomes the narrative center of a thermodynamically inspired model. Freud himself seemingly saw no difficulty in "proving" the existence of "unconscious mental processes" by pointing out the "possibility of making sense of neurotic symptoms by analytic interpretation."[94]

The mechanisms of psychoanalysis relied on methods of recognizing repression. By recognizing symptoms, the manifestation of various psychological pressures would be alleviated. Individuals were assisted in recognizing and understanding the inner workings of their own psyches, and how their psychological patterns governed their interpretations of the world. Most importantly, they were shown how those patterns affected the way they *functioned* in the world. Like posthumanism does in contemporary times, Freudian psychoanalysis sees the key to full human efficacy as dependent upon understanding our information.

Individuals were, in essence, responsible for projecting their own realities, but were unable to interpret them. Actively recognizing their systems of misinterpretation would serve to keep them "more centered." Coupled with this was the somewhat disturbing implication that, subconsciously, individuals did not *want* to be cured, and would actively seek out traumas in their present lives that somehow mirrored the traumas which they lived through in the past. Narratively speaking, it is as if individuals actively would seek out "plots" that would allow their flawed interpretations to manifest themselves, and play out according to a pre-determined "script." Unconsciously, the ego would rather relive traumatic events than deal with the possibility of facing the roots of those traumas. But, according to Freud, facing the origins of those traumas was the key to bringing an end to the symptoms which mark their absence in conscious thought.

Freud's contention that various traumatic events act as specific sources of psychological/mental pressure has a dual effect: It "quantifies" experience— casting past events (remembered and unremembered) as *information*; thus giving information a substantive quality—as if it had a weight or a mass that could only manifest itself in symptoms that required a narrative/interpretive process to be both identified and treated. This quantifiable mental "energy," while causing physical symptoms, relied on a discursive process to be identified. The psychological interpretation of information by the individual could have *physical* effects. Information now had substance.

Freud's implication that experienced events (especially events that were repressed) acted as a kind of "energy" that exerted pressure on the psyche is an important precursor to the posthuman assumption that privileges pattern over material instantiation. In more contemporary terms, traumatic information can cause repression (a subconscious forgetting of that information) which in turn can manifest itself as physical symptoms. Writing before the rise of cybernetics, Freud's conceptualization of information was limited by the scientific theories (and metaphors) of his day. Thermodynamic concepts of pressure, heat, balance, agitation, etc., represented the same quantitative effects that more contemporary concepts of information, code, data, encoding, and decoding have today. Regardless of how it is characterized, Freud's idea that an experienced event (as energy exerting pressure on the psyche or as information being processed) had "substance" anticipated its posthuman counterpart by over a century.

If the repressed traumatic information is later manifested as physical symptoms, it does so as a result of a misinterpretation. The human inevitably misinterprets information as it is experienced. In posthuman terms, we are limited in our ability to mediate the information that constitutes experience. In Freudian terms, the source of psychological and psychosomatic symptoms is a structural conflict caused by a faulty interpretation of information. Thus, the act of analysis had to be interpretive as well, needing a necessarily distanced point of view (at first by the analyst, and then, eventually by the patient) in order to *correctly* interpret the information of experience.

A more centralized point of view then allows patients to "re-experience some portion of [their] forgotten [lives], but must see to it, on the other hand, that the patient[s] retain some degree of aloofness, which will enable [them], in spite of everything, to recognize what appears to be reality is in fact only a reflection of [their] forgotten past[s]."[95] Experience is further qualified as a type of information—objectified as quantitative *data*—is able to be "taken in," "reflected," or even ignored.

Patients in need of analysis are betrayed by their inability to mediate traumatic *information* and successfully function within the world. They have lost a centrality—feeling a lack of control over the "taking in" of the events that happen around them. They can no longer trust their human ability to interpret the events around them. Their ability to experience the world has become inadequate, and, when symptoms become severe enough, they can no longer *function* in the world. Subjectivity is not so much threatened as it is displaced: instead of actively taking in the world, the individual is "pulled along" by the uninformed "taking in" of information. One can see the seed of Lyotard's own version of "complexification" here, but with less of a technological slant.

Once again, the overall effect is a general de-emphasis of the agency of the human being in light of the information which surrounds us. Our own ability to experience the world—our human means of taking in information (physically, psychologically, emotionally) is flawed and incomplete without someone (in psychoanalysis, the analyst) or something (in posthumanism, technological systems) to supplement our ability to process what we experience. Psychoanalysis places our human limitation at the site of interpretation: we cannot accurately interpret the information which we take in, thus requiring the presence of an analyst to help us re-experience and re-interpret traumatic events. Posthumanism places our limitations earlier on, at the site of experience (or enframing) itself: we require a technological supplement in order to accurately apprehend the world as it comes in.

Regardless of where the human limitation is located, the results are the same: individuals are betrayed by their inability to accurately and effectively process information, and we cannot effectively interface with the world. Yet, the way we apprehend the world (accurately or, in most cases, inaccurately) defines our existence. It places the responsibility for the creation of our realities squarely on us. In this manner, we are actually centralized and marginalized simultaneously. The characteristic "backhand" that is present in posthumanism is also present in psychoanalysis. Every action is potentially within the patient's control. The individual has the *potential* to control his or her information, and—if we think in posthuman terms—the ability to control it *at the point of its actual receiving*. Posthumanism builds on the concept of responsibility in Freud by raising the possibility (or more accurately, the hope) that, through technology, we might be able to alter the "apparatus of experience" itself, to give us a more accurate representation of what reality actually is.

But this "hope" for control is not unique to posthumanism. Underlying the inherent pessimism of Freudian theory is a submerged hope that it *is* possible for individuals to take control of their perceptions (thus giving them a "conclusion" to progress towards). As Charles Elder points out, the patient is led to "assume responsibility for certain actions that previously seemed outside of his or her control. (The concept of the unconscious, far from undermining our personal sense of responsibility, actually extends it; what formerly belonged to chance nor becomes an expression of will.)"[96]

Here we see what are the foundations of the extension of "embodied awareness" of which Hayles speaks. For the posthuman, the means to achieve such an extension of responsibility comes through technological systems, either instrumentally (the "complacent" uploading of the consciousness), or critically by re-articulating the self as an informational pattern which is both susceptible to and made more potent (ala Haraway) by the successful manipulation of information.

In Freud's system, individuals have the potential to become masters of their own fates, primarily by holding themselves up to a "prime self" characterized by a balanced (as per a thermodynamic metaphor) system. This prime self is, essentially, a technological self—a thermodynamic self that responds to information (as pressures) through self-regulation, in the same way a thermodynamic system naturally achieves stasis. Compare this to the "prime self" in Hayles and Haraway: the posthuman or the cyborg reaches an informed, ethereal awareness that has no problem mediating the boundaries between itself and the technological other.

And here is the difficulty/limitation that both theories share: has any individual reached this balanced/cyborg/posthuman self? Is it *humanly* possible to reach the "completed" subjectivity that posthumanism or psychoanalysis attempts to move toward. Returning to Freud, we can view psychoanalytic theory as one that empowers the individual by privileging the potentially well-balanced self as the central nexus of experience, but it also places a vast amount of responsibility on individuals themselves, who must not only come to terms with their theoretical role as "projectors," but also with an almost elementary, everyday contradiction: things happen.

That is to say, events happen which fall out of the realm of self-generated occurrences: a loved one falls ill; an accident occurs; the bank makes an error that causes funds to disappear. These are not things that the individual causes him or herself. We may project our worlds—therefore being responsible for their projection, but responsibility *does not* bring with it *control*. Things happen outside of the self and those occurrences are represented within our own spheres of description. While we may have no control over those events themselves, psychoanalysis points to the possibility that we may have control over how we choose to represent them—or at least, characterize the representations for which we are responsible (which are, in the strictest sense, not *actual* reality).[97]

To what end, however, does such a realization bring us? There is an inherent movement in psychoanalysis toward some kind of narrative aspect of conclusion—whether it is the overcoming of all repression, the cessation of symptoms, and/or the ability of patients to successfully interact with the world around them—*thus allowing them to move on*. But, problems can arise when the model one is "concluding toward" is based upon a technological concept of completion. The completion of analysis *should* consist of a total reorientation of patients, allowing them to more successfully interpret the "information" of their daily lives—lives free from the absences which they were forced to fill. The gaps have been filled in, and balance has been achieved.

But as Freud found out, it was not that simple. Symptoms recurred, repression resurfaced, and a current, new trauma could test the "revised" narrative that the patient and analyst has created. Furthermore, analysis itself could bring about entirely new traumas that would then have to be dealt with recursively. While it is the *point* of psychoanalysis to recreate existing traumas via transference, these traumas are rooted in the past. The inability of classic psychoanalysis to deal directly with a new trauma that might present itself either during or after analysis was terminated became an increasingly troublesome issue during Freud's time, calling into question the overall effectiveness of psychoanalysis. It was becoming increasingly evident that the inherent discord between the goals and results of analysis was calling into question its ability to "cure" or, for that matter, what "to be cured" even meant. Freud sought to address these issues in "Analysis Terminable and Interminable."

"Analysis Terminable and Interminable": Narrative Conclusions versus Technological Completion

Written in 1937, "Analysis Terminable and Interminable" becomes a study in the inherent conflict between the practical and theoretical (and the narrative and technological) aspects of Freudian theory.[98] The theoretical Freud maintains that analysis should conclude when: a) the patient no longer suffers from his former symptoms and has "overcome his various anxieties and inhibitions"; and b) *The analyst* has "formed the opinion that so much repressed material has been brought into consciousness, so much that was inexplicable elucidated, and so much inner resistance overcome that no repetition of the patient's specific pathological process is to be feared."[99] This would represent a true completion of analysis marked by a saturation of analysis.

Yet, toward the conclusion of the essay, a more practical voice arises: "The business of analysis is to secure the best possible psychological conditions for the ego; when this has been done, analysis has accomplished its task."[100] Here, Freud characterizes the end of analysis as more of a conclusion that is to be enacted. One can sense Freud's attempt to find a characterization of conclusion that included the attainment of a specific mental "state," thus ending the process of analysis. But even this is tenuous. Securing the best possible psychological conditions is not a one-time-only event, but would instead have to be an ongoing process. The summary statement "the business of analysis" illustrates a begrudging compromise between the more theoretical/technological goals of completion and the more practical/narrative goal of conclusion. These two sometimes opposing currents in the essay are indicative of an underlying dissonance in Freudian theory.

At the start of the essay, Freud relates his own attempts to shorten analysis in the case of Sergei Pankejeff, a.k.a. the "Wolfman," but only because he felt it was a "case of the treatment obstructing itself" and that the process of analysis was on the verge of "failure."[101] The "heroic remedy" of imposing an end to treatment was taken as a last resort. Faced with stagnating analysis, Freud imposed an arbitrary "end point," or conclusion, to the analysis. He informed Pankejeff that analysis would be terminated at a specific time no matter how much progress was (or wasn't) made—something Freud himself called "blackmail."[102]

Freud's more practical decision of imposing a conclusion alludes to a certain betrayal that occurred between Freud's theoretical and interpretive notions of "cure." When the analysis of Pankejeff failed to stay in line with his theoretical expectations for a "balanced equation," Freud seems to defer to a more narrative approach by establishing a conclusion to move the analysis toward. Whether one is directly imposed or is simply assumed to exist, the presence of a conclusion provided Pankejeff with *a* goal (as opposed to *the* goal) to move toward. The imposed conclusion would (hopefully) serve to as the necessary boundary which would contain—or at least limit—the scope of Pankejeff's analysis.

The "threat" of an ending (albeit an imposed one) seemed to be an initial success. Freud maintained that the resistances "crumble[d] away" and that Pankejeff was "able to produce all the memories and . . . discover the connecting links which were necessary for the understanding of his early neurosis and his recovery from the illness from which he was suffering."[103] As time passed, however, Pankejeff suffered numerous relapses, thus potentially embarrassing Freud because he was "still in Vienna talking to people."[104] Although Freud at first believed that his cure was "complete and permanent,"[105] he later admitted that he had been mistaken concerning his approach with Pankejeff, but rather than directly fault his methods, Freud instead implied that certain stressful events in Pankejeff's life might have been responsible for reviving "offshoots of his original neurosis."[106] It would seem that the completion Freud was looking for was foiled by temporality itself.

Pankejeff's case was frustrating to Freud for more reasons than one, but the root of his frustration alludes to the manner in which his classic psychoanalytic approach was unable to "make room for" traumatic events which occurred in the present moment. Pankejeff's own circumstances at the time were stressful in and of themselves, and to Freud, it was those, more current, stressful events which were actually serving as an impediment to the process of analysis.[107] Pankejeff's life was literally getting in the way.

Freud was faced with the fact that Pankejeff's psyche was not the closed thermodynamic-like system that psychoanalytic theory presented. A constant influx of events caused an instability that could not be fully compensated for. The events of everyday life interfered with the balance that was theoretically possible. The human condition—the manner in which we experience the temporality of the world—seemed to contaminate the conditions of the more closed system of psychoanalysis. Again, we see the limitations of the physical human. It is no wonder that in more contemporary terms, information is seen as "pure," but, when handled by imperfect human beings, can often be "corrupted."[108] This is why Haraway's cyborg is "clean and ethereal," and Hayles' posthuman is free of the limitations of the liberal humanist subject. For Freud, his attempts to bring Pankejeff to a state of completion were corrupted by the very condition of Pankejeff's humanity.

Analysis—and the anamnesis that take place during analysis—worked most successfully in dealing with the past. Freud states that "the work of analysis progresses best when the patient's pathogenic experiences belong to the past so that the ego can stand at a distance from them. In conditions of acute crisis, it is, to all intents and purposes, impossible to use analysis."[109] Thus, analysis becomes ineffective at dealing with a crisis of the "here and now," since a necessary distance between originary traumatic events and the patient him or herself must be established.

The groundbreaking theories, the complex "mapping" of the psyche, and even the process of transference are—*in a strictly scientific/theoretical sense*—rendered useless in dealing with a present trauma that is not the result of the analysis itself.[110] Current traumas did not fit into Freud's "system." At best, the patient might be made aware of the pattern of his coping strategies, but if the patient were to suffer an acute trauma in the present moment, the Freudian analytic process would become impossible to carry out: "In such states the whole interest of the ego is concentrated on the painful reality, and resists analysis, which seeks to penetrate below the surface and to discover the influences to which the patient has been exposed to in the past."[111]

It would seem that for analysis to come to an effective conclusion, the patient would have to be completely free of any major traumas that might occur in his or her daily life.[112] Again, Freud's theoretical expectations are betrayed by "real world" events, thwarting a theoretical completion. At best, he—and his patients—could only aspire to a theoretical (and scientifically informed) notion of completion.

Freud's stressing of conclusion to "force an end" of analysis is echoed in posthumanism's attempts to conclude humanism. Whether critically (through anamnesis as characterized by Badmington) or uncritically (through an abandonment of the body), posthumanism implies that the problems associated with the human (the liberal humanist subject and/or the physical body) will somehow disappear when the posthuman state is achieved.

It seems at times as if Freud himself was unable to come to terms with the question of "conclusion" regarding analysis. However, Freud still defended his actions in terms of Pankejeff's case, with reservations: "There can be one verdict about the value of this blackmailing device. The measure is effective, provided that one hits the right time at which to employ it. But it cannot be held to guarantee the perfect accomplishment of the task of psychoanalysis."[113] Later, Freud asks "is there such a thing as a natural end to analysis or is it really possible to conduct it to such an end?"[114]

While the more pragmatic answer is an optimistic one, one in which the patient is brought to a functional state, being "cured enough" to live his life with the possibility of some relapses, Freud also advanced a more theoretical response, one in which a true cure seems more unattainable. To achieve a more "ambitious" goal to the end of analysis, Freud maintained that treatment would have to be

> so profound that no further change would take place in him if his analysis would be continued. The implication is that by means of analysis it is possible to attain to absolute physical normality and to be sure that it will be maintained, the supposition being that all the patient's repressions have been lifted and every gap in his memory filled.[115]

If the analyst were to adhere to this "ambitious" answer to the question of the cessation of analysis, it would require the analysis itself to be *constant* and *lifelong*. There would have to be a constant presence and continuous guidance of the analyst to help patients integrate the unfolding events of their lives with the traumas of the past, which simultaneously must be kept in check. The patient would have to be saturated with analysis. This, of course, is impossible. Practically speaking, Freud can only gesture toward balance which, conversely, opens up the possibility for perpetual improvement. If we cannot achieve absolute physical normalcy, we can at least strive toward it—until we die trying.

This opens up another, more latent, aspect of posthumanism which is related to Lyotard's and Heidegger's ideas of progress. The human desire to constantly uncover information, sparked by the faith of the inexhaustibility of the perceivable, represents a constant striving. It is not clear whether or not posthumanism is the manifestation of that striving, or if it is an imposed conclusion to that striving. Are we seeking, as a technological species, to finally "come to rest" by transcending the need for technology? Or does posthumanism represent an unconscious desire to hold onto an aspect of the human in light of dehumanizing technologies, setting up a "perpetual humanism" that will remain regardless of our technological progress?

Perhaps, in the end, the posthuman is aware of the impossibility of "full embodied awareness," just as Freud was aware that true completion of analysis was impossible. If the posthuman "knows" that the goal it is looking for is impossible, then the perpetual striving toward that goal is a way to maintain the viability of the human subject in light of technological development. Neither critical nor complacent posthumanism seeks a total destruction of the subject. Each, ultimately, seeks an *improvement* of it—whether through a transcendence that nullifies the need for the technological other (thus making a "perfect," saturated subjectivity), or through an uploading that overcomes the physical limitations of the prosthetic body. Achieving the posthuman would be the end of the human. Implying that this state is an impossible perfection once again brings us back to the idea that technology itself has been transformed (according to Scarry's model) into a superior other, but still protects the "specialness" of the human by characterizing us as dutifully striving for improvement.[116]

Returning momentarily to Freud, we see that while fully cured individuals should be able to maintain such balances on their own, even the most balanced individual, one who displays no more symptoms that call for analysis, runs the risk of relapse: "it still, of course, remains an open question how much of this immunity is due to a benevolent fate which spares him too searching a test."[117] It is ironic that a theory which, according to Breger, "abolished" fate, ultimately relies on it to keep its patients healthy.

Thus, even the most balanced individuals are constantly poised on the edge of further repression and subsequent symptoms; yet there is always room for improvement. Freud acknowledges the skepticism that such a conclusion might incur, but then implies that time is the ruling factor regarding the "success" of analysis, and that even if the patient seems totally "cured" and thus can be said to have completed their analysis, there is no way to predict if the "cure" will hold from decade to decade, or even year to year. The individual always holds the potential to improve, progress, and move forward. Within the skepticism of psychoanalysis lies a subtle hopefulness that we can—at least—attempt to move *toward* a specific goal, albeit a created one.

"Progress" here is not based on a constant uncovering of information as it is perceived, but in a process of anamnesis which seeks to situate the individual in such a way as to make him or her ready—and better prepared—to take in the experiences (information) which he or she is exposed to every day. Technologically speaking, the difficulty comes in when we are not able to successfully process the information which we uncover. Rather than effectively use the information we gain, we instead simply "store it" (in a Heideggerian sense) for future use—even though we have no idea what that use might be.

A very simple example here would be to think of e-mail. How many old e-mail messages are in our inboxes? How many copies of sent items reside in our "sent items" folders? How often do we "purge" those folders? For some, they are never purged. There is a constant nagging feeling that at some point we might *need* that information. There is a security in knowing that it is there, even though we know that we have limited storage capacity and that thousands of saved e-mail messages might be slowing down our systems. In a fit of rage or even in a desire to "uncomplicate" things, we delete them all. Until, inevitably, that *one* message in the thousands we deleted was one we could have used.[118]

But the anxiety of deletion here often pales in comparison to the anxiety of the "uncovering" itself. I speak here of the obsessive e-mail checker, whose e-mail application is set to check for messages every five minutes, or who cannot undertake any task without first checking their e-mail. If we find ourselves in that classification, what are we expecting to receive? Is there a specific message we might get that will quench that need to keep checking for the day? If the answer is an honest yes, then we are indeed using technology for a specific purpose. But if their answer is a hesitant "no," then we are in the midst of a posthuman suffering, obsessively and blindly staggering forward (as Lyotard illustrates), for something we wouldn't recognize even if we could grasp it.

Indeed, Freud could not have envisioned the technological advancements that would occur after his lifetime, but that is not to say that he was not sensitive to the pressures of technology that existed in his own time. Technology had made possible the scientific innovations in the field of thermodynamics which so influenced Freud's thinking. In those models, Freud saw a means to make sense of the mysteries of the human psyche. It was a clean, simple, and efficient system which represented the possibility of balance.

But it was the "efficiency" of the system which eventually worked against Freud. The human being itself worked *against* such efficiency. And, on a completely other level, it was the *expectation of efficiency* which eventually haunted Freud and caused him frustration—not only in his own attempts at analysis, but also in how *others* attempted to apply his theories. Freud was becoming increasingly annoyed by European, and especially American, attempts to accelerate analysis, the practice of which he attributes mainly to Otto Rank as symptomatic of a desire to make psychoanalysis better "suit the rush of American life."[119] It would seem that the progress made possible by technological development was a double-edged sword, one which is still being brought to bear today in posthumanism.

Psychoanalysis, Posthumanism, and the Other

Psychoanalysis and posthumanism have at their cores the goal of overcoming their own necessity. More specifically, each seeks a way to overcome the need for the supplemental other upone which each relies. The process of psychoanalysis would not be possible without the presence of the analyst as the separate "other" point of view which helps patients re-establish themselves as the center of their own psychological narrative. Posthumanism, especially critical posthumanism, relies on the presence of a technological other which helps individuals attain a better relationship with their defining information. The perfectly balanced, fully realized individual in psychoanalytic theory transcends the need for the analyst, just as the fully realized posthuman transcends the need for technology.

Each also shares the belief that through recognition, understanding, and knowledge, the mental and physical condition of the human can be altered for the better. If we cultivate a better awareness of how we process information, then we can become more effective human beings. For Freud, we become the person we were meant to be—one that was no longer at the mercy of repressed traumas. For the posthuman, we reach our fully embodied potentials, and are able to interface with the information around us without the need of a separate technological artifact.

But more than simply drawing a comparison, we can also look to posthumanism as a progression of psychoanalytic theory as well, especially when we take into consideration our earlier discussion of the work of Elaine Scarry and her ideas regarding human invention as, essentially, expressions of pain. In many ways, technological invention can also be viewed as a "symptom," where technological systems and artifacts become instantiated marks of trauma and repression.

In Freudian psychoanalysis, physical symptoms are manifestations of externalized psychological pain. According to Scarry, pain brings the body to the forefront at the cost of the outside world—we externalize the pain we feel by "making" artifacts or "making marks" as an attempt to make that pain available to others, essentially creating a perfect record of—or witness to—that pain. In psychoanalysis, the analyst attempts to be a "perfect witness" to the pain individuals are experiencing. The main difficulty arises in that the very presence of the analyst—while on the surface, a beneficial one—is still a reminder that the patient cannot achieve relief alone. The individual is still inadequate and incomplete and requires the supplement of the analyst to achieve relief. Returning to Scarry, no matter how effective the artifact is, it still becomes a mark of our own incompleteness.

In "Analysis Terminable and Interminable," Freud attempts to come to terms with the fact that to achieve perfect analysis, the analyst would have to remain as a constant presence in the patient's life, and even that would not guarantee that the patient could remain balanced in light of new traumas. Hence the compromise of analysis just having to be "effective enough" to get the patient to a functional state. Freud ultimately acknowledged the human condition itself: one that was susceptible to the condition of its own temporality.

Posthumanism has not yet reached that point. Even as it names anamnesis as a possible alternative to the complexification of experience, it still does so as a means to an end, rather than as an ongoing process. Psychoanalytic theory acknowledged the narrativity of human experience which Lyotard points out, while posthumanism represses it. There still seems to be a belief that there *will be a time* when we can achieve the perfect interface with information. If psychoanalysis were to ignore the realities of a "cure" in the same manner as posthumanism ignores the realities of "full embodied awareness," it would be searching for the *perfect analyst*—the analyst who could perform the perfect analysis that would obliterate all repression, re-integrate the individual, and allow the individual to *completely* overcome the current (and any future) need for the analyst him or herself. Most importantly, it would then state that only then could the individual "move on" and live.

Both psychoanalytic theory and posthumanism rely on a concept of a superior other in order to reach their conclusions. The other in psychoanalytic theory, however, is human and imperfect, but does not need to be perfect in order to help a patient. The analyst, while highly skilled and having been analyzed him or herself, is superior primarily in his or her *position* in relation to the traumas of the patient. Psychoanalytic theory even takes into account the limitations of the analyst by bringing up the possibility of countertransference (the surfacing of the analysts' own repressed feelings as analysis takes place).

Posthumanism, however, has yet to come to terms with the supplementarity of technology as a created superior other. It has yet to recognize the nature of that other, which is, in reality, a reflected human subjectivity—one which the posthuman believes to be perfect because of its pure technicity. Posthumanism itself is suffering from a vast repression. The question is, what was the original trauma that could have caused such a repression? What is the nature of the "profound injury" which Haraway spoke about in her "Cyborg Manifesto"?

As already discussed, as technology advances (especially in the manner characterized by Lyotard), we—as humans—become more distanced from it. The skill required to use it is "built out" in its complexification. Using psychoanalytic theory as an example, we are like the patient who has distanced him or herself from a traumatic event, and have fallen victim to the gaps in memory that the repression has opened up. We become blind to the causes of those repressions. They take over, and our bodies (and minds) respond in ways we do not understand.

Psychoanalytic theory asks us to successfully "embrace" the trauma, and attempt to (borrowing a phrase from Heidegger), get it in hand. We do so by establishing (with the help of the analyst) a viable point of view. We re-organize and re-establish our personal narratives in order to re-incorporate the memories of forgotten traumatic events. In so many ways, Haraway and Hayles seem to be attempting to do the same thing, but they are attempting to do so without knowing what the original trauma was/is in the first place. That trauma is the original giving over of our own superiority, and is also the original separation between the human and the technological artifact.

The reason why posthumanism does not address the actual site of interface between human and technological system is because it is the site of the "profound injury" which Haraway identifies. If technology is ultimately an expression of pain, and a mark of the suffering which occurs in the inability to share pain, then our human attempt to extend our influence into the world through a technological artifact becomes a re-playing of the original trauma of our original inability to share that pain. We attempt to use technology in order to overcome the trauma caused by technology in the first place.

While this may sound perverse, it is actually not very different from Freudian psychoanalysis. A trauma is suffered because of a faulty interpretation of events. Our narratives are thus flawed. Through psychoanalysis, we use the very same means—narrative interpretation—to work through repression and trauma. For Freud, we take in the world narratively, thus to undo the damage created by our faulty perceptions and re-integrate ourselves with the narrative experience we create, we must use narrative. In posthumanist terms, if we take in the world technologically, then we must seek a technological integration with that world.

Is this simply a re-articulation of psychoanalytic theory in technological terms? Not exactly. What makes posthumanism unique is the significance placed on information. For Freud, information (as experience) had power in its characterization as a force. It had a certain substantive quality in its ability to produce change. However, the re-conceptualization of information presented by Hayles gives information an actual presence—a power that is based on its ability to produce physical systems (i.e., the human body as a direct expression of genetic code). Information is rendered "real." This change in the idea of what information actually was had a profound effect on the significance we give to information itself. Code had presence. It was no longer a case of manipulating information as a force. With the right techniques, information can be manipulated to directly produce *things*.

Programming a computer can create actual results. The code we "feed it" will cause a direct change in what that machine does. As technology, especially digital technology, becomes more ubiquitous, the power of code becomes more significant.[120] More specifically, this reconceptualization of code changed what had significance. The information that was "behind" technological artifacts was actually the same information that was "behind" the human being—and experience—itself. Remember, the posthuman condition maintains that information can freely pass from substrate to substrate. As technology advances, and various systems and artifacts become more independent, we—as humans—become more distanced from those systems in terms of the human skill required to effect change, thus, paradoxically exacerbating our feelings of inadequacy.

Posthumanism has yet to come to terms with the "instrumentality" that Heidegger points out. We see our tools as the way to make a "mark" in the world, and we invest faith in them through our belief that they can extend our reach. Thus, to extend our reach even further—to get more "power"—we must have more complex and powerful tools to make bigger marks in the world. But this only makes things worse: the greater the mark, the greater the distance between the limited physical human and the mark that has been made.

It is no wonder that posthumanism calls for an "embrace" of the technology; it becomes a way to project our own human frailties upon technological systems, since, according to Scarry, we often see superior, god-like systems as immune to the things that humans themselves are susceptible to. But the embrace that posthumanism espouses is actually a repression of the trauma of the initial need for technology. The embrace is a symptom of our own internal feelings of inadequacy and incompleteness. We embrace our technology as an attempt to get technology back in hand; as an attempt to re-incorporate the externalized efficacy which technological instruments represent.

This would explain why critical posthumanism views anamnesis as a means to an end, rather than as an ongoing process. The desire to embrace technology blinds the posthuman to the nature of the relationship itself: that technology, ontologically speaking, *is* the defining characteristic of life. That we *narratively* attempt to make sense out of information is what makes us human. Although Hayles does point out the general power we invest in technology, she does *not* take into consideration the personal *significance* we place on information.

Critical posthumanism is not enough to better mediate our relationship to technology, because it relies too heavily on instrumentality. It keeps looking for an "other" in terms of a specific apparatus, rather than at the "other" as a manifestation of our own human frailties as the symptom of the use of technology itself. If we are being "pulled forward" by complexification, it is because we do not recognize the "essence" of technology. Badmington's desire to engage in anamnesis is actually a noble effort, in that he is calling for a pause to try and understand why we are being pulled forward in the first place. Unfortunately, the belief that anamnesis can be achieved technologically actually causes a speeding up of complexification itself.

Notes

1. Neil Badmington, "Theorizing Posthumanism," *Cultural Critique* 53 (2003): 11.
2. Although Lyotard and Freud will be dealt with more directly later in the chapter, anamnesis here implies a guided remembering or recollection, literally "to put in mind" (*mimneeskein*) "again" (*ana*), to gain an eventual "working through."
3. Badmington, "Theorizing Posthumanism," 15.
4. Badmington, "Theorizing Posthumanism," 16.
5. Rene Descartes, *Discourse on the Method of Rightly Conducting One's Reason and Seeking the Truth in the Sciences*, in *Descartes: Selected Philosophical Writings*, ed. and trans. John Cottingham, Robert Stoothoff, and Dugald Murdoch, 20-56. Cambridge: Cambridge University Press, 1988, 20 quoted in Badmington, "Theorizing Posthumanism," 16-17.
6. Badmington, "Theorizing Posthumanism," 16.
7. Descartes, *Discourse*, 36, qtd. in Badmington, "Theorizing Posthumanism," 17.
8. Badmington, "Theorizing Posthumanism," 17.
9. Rene Descartes, *Meditations on First Philosophy in Which are Demonstrated the Existence of God and the Distinction between the Human Soul and the Body*, in *Descartes: Selected Philosophical Writings*, ed. and trans. John Cottingham, Robert Stoothoff, and Dugald Murdoch, 73-122. Cambridge: Cambridge University Press, 1988, 120, quoted in Badmington, "Theorizing Posthumanism," 17.
10. Descartes, *Meditations*, 120, qtd. in Badmington, "Theorizing Posthumanism," 17.
11. Badmington, "Theorizing Posthumanism," 17.
12. A posthuman perspective views every aspect of the body as a physically instantiated expression of our genetic codes. How we develop physically (eye color, intelligence, height, life span) is basically an "executed" code.
13. The clearest example of this would be Stanley Kubrick's film adaptation of Arthur C. Clark's *2001: A Space Odyssey*, where David Bowman achieves transcendence through mastering and eventually overcoming the technological systems that both assist

and threaten him, only to become "reborn" as a form represented by a human embryo floating in space. Another, more contemporary example would be Neo from the *Matrix* films, who eventually is able to manipulate technology in the dystopian "real world" without any interface, by simply thinking about it, or extending his hand.

14. Assuming that information could travel freely across material substrates, not only could the consciousness as a pattern of info be uploaded, but it could also be susceptible to corruption or deletion as well.

15. "Secondly, even though they might do some things as well as or even better than we do them, they would inevitably fail in others, through which we would discover that they were acting not through understanding [*connaissance*] but only from the disposition of their organs. For whereas reason is a universal instrument which can be of use in all kinds of situations, these organs need some particular disposition for each particular action; hence it is impossible to conceive that there would be enough of them in a machine to make it act in all the occurrences of life in the way in which our reason makes us act." Descartes, *Discourse on Method*, trans. Badmington (44–45), qtd. in Badmington, "Theorizing Posthumanism," 18.

16. Badmington, "Theorizing Posthumanism," 18.

17. Badmington, "Theorizing Posthumanism," 19.

18. Badmington, "Theorizing Posthumanism," 22.

19. Badmington, "Theorizing Posthumanism," 23.

20. Martin Heidegger, "The Question Concerning Technology," *The Question Concerning Technology and Other Essays*, trans. William Lovitt, (New York: Harper & Row, 1977), 12.

21. According to translator William Lovitt, "Essence is the traditional translation of the German noun Wesen . . . which does not simply mean what something is, but what it means, further, the way in which something pursues its course, the way in which it remains through time as what it is." *The Question Concerning Technology and Other Essays*, 3.

22. Again, in terms of the German *wesen*, which, in this case is translated as a verb "to come to presence," "a rendering wherein the meaning 'endure' should be strongly heard." Lovitt, *The Question Concerning Technology and Other Essays*, 4.

23. Heidegger, "The Question Concerning Technology," 4.

24. Heidegger, "The Question Concerning Technology," 4.

25. Heidegger, "The Question Concerning Technology," 5.

26. Heidegger, "The Question Concerning Technology," 10-11.

27. Scarry, *Body in Pain*, 125.

28. Heidegger, "The Question Concerning Technology," 13.

29. Heidegger, "The Question Concerning Technology," 14. According to Lovitt, *Herausfordern* "means to challenge, to call forth or summon to action, to demand positively, to provoke," *The Question Concerning Technology and Other Essays*, 14.

30. Heidegger, "The Question Concerning Technology," 14.

31. Heidegger, "The Question Concerning Technology," 14-15.

32. Heidegger, "The Question Concerning Technology," 15.

33. Heidegger, "The Question Concerning Technology," 16.

34. Heidegger, "The Question Concerning Technology," 17. Lovitt notes "*Bestand* ordinarily denotes a store or supply as 'standing by.' It carries the connotation of the verb *bestehen* with its dual meaning of to last and to undergo. Heidegger uses the word to characterize the manner in which everything commanded into place and ordered according to the challenging demand ruling in modern technology presences as revealed. He

wishes to stress here not the permanency, but the orderability and substitutablity of objects." *The Question Concerning Technology and Other Essays*, 17.

35. Although some elements found on the Periodic Table are man-made (all elements with an atomic number greater than 92), these elements are "created" by manipulating the atomic structures of pre-existing elements on the quantum level. This is another aspect of "setting in order" which Heidegger discusses.

36. John Zuern, "Martin Heidegger: The Question Concerning Technology," *Criticalink*, University of Hawaii at Manoa, http://www2.hawaii.edu/~zuern/demo/Heidegger (Accessed August 8, 2005).

37. Heidegger, "The Question Concerning Technology," 19.

38. "We now name that challenging claim which gathers man thither to order the self-revealing as standing-reserve: 'Ge-stell' [Enframing]," Heidegger, "The Question Concerning Technology," 19. According to Lovitt, "The translation 'Enframing' for *Gestell* is intended to suggest, through the use of the prefix 'en-,' something of the active meaning that Heidegger here gives to the German word." Lovitt warns the reader that the word does not simply mean a "framework of some sort." Instead, we "should constantly remember that Enframing is fundamentally a calling-forth. It is a 'challenging claim,' a demanding summons, that 'gathers' so as to reveal. This claim enframes in that it assembles and orders." *The Question Concerning Technology and Other Essays*, 19.

39. Heidegger, "The Question Concerning Technology," 21.

40. Heidegger, "The Question Concerning Technology," 23 (emphasis mine).

41. Zuern, "Martin Heidegger."

42. Heidegger, "The Question Concerning Technology," 24.

43. Zuern, "Martin Heidegger."

44. Heidegger, "The Question Concerning Technology," 25-26.

45. Heidegger, "The Question Concerning Technology," 28.

46. Heidegger, "The Question Concerning Technology," 33.

47. Heidegger, "The Question Concerning Technology," 34.

48. Zuern, "Martin Heidegger."

49. Although it may seem odd to worry about an event that will happen so far away from us in time, the fact serves as an "ultimate conclusion" to humanity.

50. Jean-François Lyotard, *The Inhuman: Reflections on Time*, trans. Geoffrey Benningtong and Rachel Bowlby (Stanford: Stanford University Press, 1991), 12.

51. Lyotard, *The Inhuman*, 12.

52. "A human, in short, is a living organization that is not only complex but, so to speak, replex. It can grasp itself as a medium . . . or as an organ . . . or as an object. It can even abstract itself from itself and take into account only its rules of processing, as in logic and mathematics." Lyotard, *The Inhuman*, 12.

53. Hayles, *Posthuman*, 2.

54. Lyotard, *The Inhuman*, 62.

55. Lyotard, *The Inhuman*, 53.

56. Lyotard, *The Ihumhan*, 15-16.

57. Paul Harris, "Thinking @ the Speed of Time: Globalization and Its Discontents, or Can Lyotard's Thought Go on Without a Body?" *Yale French Studies* 99 (2001): 133.

58. Harris, "Thinking @ the Speed of Time," 133-34.

59. Harris, "Thinking @ the Speed of Time," 130.

60. Harris, "Thinking @ the Speed of Time, 130-31.

61. It is tempting here to characterize complexification as simply an inundation of information. However, complexification actually implies the attempt of the system to

respond to the information that is coming in. The system must be able to use and incorporate the information which is coming in.

62. Lyotard, *The Inhuman*, 22.

63. Lyotard, *The Inhuman*, 46.

64. Lyotard, *The Inhuman*, 45.

65. Lyotard, *The Inhuman*, 45.

66. Lyotard, *The Inhuman*, 62. Lyotard specifically speaks to "communicational development" here, especially as a method of what he calls an "extended memory" which would allow humans to store the vast amount of information which is being uncovered.

67. Lyotard, *The Inhuman*, 62.

68. "And if the exodus succeeds, what it will have preserved is not the species itself but the 'most complete monad' with which it was pregnant." Lyotard, *The Inhuman*, 65. The "most complete monad" Lyotard speaks of is a reference to the metaphysical philosophy of Leibniz, whose concept of "monads" were the smallest, indivisible, elemental units of substance. Applied to complacent posthumanism, the monad would be the elemental "human" aspect that would survive the uploading of consciousness into a machine.

69. Lyotard, *The Inhuman*, 63.

70. Lyotard, *The Inhuman*, 64.

71. Lyotard, *The Inhuman*, 2.

72. Harris, "Thinking @ the Speed of Time," 131.

73. Lyotard, *The Inhuman*, 16.

74. Lyotard, *The Inhuman*, 16.

75. Lyotard, *The Inhuman*, 17.

76. Lyotard, *The Inhuman*, 17.

77. Lyotard, *The Inhuman*, 17.

78. Lyotard, *The Inhuman*, 17.

79. Lyotard, *The Inhuman*, 18.

80. Lyotard, *The Inhuman*, 18.

81. Lyotard, *The Inhuman*, 18.

82. Scarry, *The Body in Pain*, 22.

83. Lyotard, *The Inhuman*, 19.

84. Harris, "Thinking @ the Speed of Time," 137.

85. Peter Nicholls, "Divergences: Modernism, Postmodernism, Jameson and Lyotard," *Critical Quarterly* 33.3 (1991): 5.

86. Harris, "Thinking @ the Speed of Time," 140.

87. Lyotard, *The Inhuman*, 54.

88. Harris, "Thinking @ the Speed of Time," 141.

89. Harris, "Thinking @ the Speed of Time," 140.

90. Harris, "Thinking @ the Speed of Time," 141.

91. Lyotard, *The Inhuman*, 63.

92. Badmington, "Theorizing Posthumanism," 22-23.

93. "It is possible to have serious reservations about Freud's conception of anamnesis, and I confess I have such reservations in one sense. The fact remains that . . . the writings on psychoanalytical technique . . . teach what technology must be when the aim is to make passing or anamnesis possible." Lyotard, *The Inhuman*, 56.

94. Sigmund Freud, "Introductory Lectures on Psychoanalysis," *The Standard Edition of the Complete Psychological Works of Sigmund Freud*, ed. and trans. James Strachey et al., Vols 15-16 (London: Hogarth Press, 1953-74), 345-46.

95. Sigmund Freud, "Beyond the Pleasure Principle," *The Standard Edition of the Complete Psychological Works of Sigmund Freud*, ed. and trans. James Strachey et al., Vol 18 (London: Hogarth Press, 1953-74), 19. Through the process of transference, the patient re-experiences the trauma associated with the formerly repressed events, but this time does so self-consciously: "We have succeeded in reviving the old conflict which led to repression and in bringing up for revision the process that was then decided. The new material that we produce includes, first, the reminder that the earlier decision led to illness and the promise that a different path will lead to recovery, and, secondly the enormous change in all the circumstances that has taken place since the time of the original rejection." "Introductory Lectures," 544. The patient experiences "real" trauma, but in relation to a "virtual" and reconstructed experience in order to come to terms with the original trauma that caused the repression in the first place. "Thereafter it is not incorrect to say that we are no longer concerned with the patient's earlier illness but with a newly created and transformed neurosis which has taken the former's place. We have followed this new edition of the old disorder from the start, we have observed its origin and growth, and we are especially well able to find our way about in it since, as its object, we are situated at its very centre." "Introductory Lectures," 552.

96. Charles Elder, *The Grammar of the Unconscious* (University Park PA: The Pennsylvania State University Press, 1994), 149.

97. Here, psychoanalysis also shares another basic assumption with posthumanism: consciousness as an epiphenomenon. Consciousness, in both psychoanalytic theory and posthumanism is characterized as the central "processor" which attempts to take in experience as information.

98. In 1937, it seemed as if Freud himself was suffering from a need to bring a sense of conclusion to his own theories. Being two years away from death, dogged by failing health, "defecting" proteges, and his unwilling relocation as a result of the inevitability of the upcoming Second World War, Freud seemed at an apt concluding point of his own narrative. He was also facing—somewhat reluctantly—the reality of the interpretation of his theories by younger European and American practitioners who, according to Breger, were more inclined to look for solid results. Louis Breger, *Freud: Darkness in the Midst of Vision* (New York: John Wiley & Sons, Inc., 2000), 366-68. Otto Rank and his desire to shorten analysis especially draws Freud out in the essay, and exemplifies the growing desire among some of his followers for a more economical and succinct psychoanalytic process. It would seem that psychoanalysis was—like any scientific enterprise—coming under the more contemporary expectation that the process itself could be refined, shortened, and made more efficient.

99. Sigmund Freud, "Analysis Terminable and Interminable," *The Standard Edition of the Complete Psychological Works of Sigmund Freud*, ed. and trans. James Strachey et al., Vol 23 (London: Hogarth Press, 1953-74), 320.

100. Freud, "Analysis Terminable and Interminable," 354.

101. Freud, "Analysis Terminable and Interminable," 317.

102. Freud, "Analysis Terminable and Interminable," 319.

103. Freud, "Analysis Terminable and Interminable," 318.

104. The Wolfman was one of Freud's four published cases, one of only two where treatment was considered successful, and the only patient of Freud's who was still alive, "this was *the* case that purportedly demonstrated the curative power of psychoanalysis." Breger, *Freud*, 367, (emphasis his).

105. Freud, "Analysis Terminable and Interminable," 318.

106. "When, toward the end of the war, he returned to Vienna, a refugee and destitute, I had to help him to master a part of the transference which had remained unre-

solved. Within a few months this was successfully accomplished and I was able to conclude my postscript with the statement that 'since the patient has felt normal and has
behaved unexceptionally, in spite of the war having robbed him of his home, his posses-
sions, and all his family relationships.' Fifteen years have passed since then, but this verdict has not proved erroneous, though certain reservations have to be made. The patient
has remained in Vienna and has made good, although in a humble social position. Several
times, however, during this period, his satisfactory state of health has broken down, and
the attacks of neurotic illness from which he has suffered could be construed only as
offshoots of his original neurosis." Freud, "Analysis Terminable and Interminable," 318.

107. A "cured" patient is still susceptible to a recurrence of symptoms rooted in the
patient's original repression that is brought about by an entirely new trauma. In the case
of Pankejeff, Freud leaves open the possibility that his relapses were in some way caused
by Pankejeff's reduction from Russian nobility to a "humble social position."

108. Although computers do have a tendency to "corrupt" our files, more often than
not, we tend to attribute such acts back to human error itself. If we "lose" our information, we are guilty of not backing it up in the first place. Or, if our computers malfunction, we attribute their poor performance to "human error" during manufacture. We can
also see this in the early programming term "GIGO"—garbage in, garbage out: if the
program was coded improperly by the programmer, the computer would malfunction.

109. Freud, "Analysis Terminable and Interminable," 334.

110. That is not to say that psychoanalysis is not an effective method of therapy.
However, if we were to hold the psychoanalytic process to a strictly scientific model,
then it is ineffective in its inability to render the completion it seems to strive for.

111. Freud, "Analysis Terminable and Interminable," 334.

112. Not only does it become evident that Freudian psychoanalysis is ineffective
with dealing with current traumas, it becomes obvious (even to Freud) that psychoanalysis at the time could not feasibly be used as a prophylactic with which to prevent further
traumas. While Freud does allude to the fact that it might be possible to introduce the
idea of a future conflict in the patient, thereby inducing a traumatic reaction in order to
strengthen the patient's ability to deal with the possible trauma (much in the same way
vaccines introduce the very disease they are defending against into the system of the individual (ATI 334), it becomes difficult to envision how this could be accomplished
without causing the patient undue stress.

113. Freud, "Analysis Terminable and Interminable," 319. Perhaps it is this acknowledgement that causes Breger to characterize the essay as "pessimistic," and evident
that Freud was coming to realize that "the limitations of analysis clearly outweighed the
possibilities." Breger, *Freud*, 365.

114. Freud, "Analysis Terminable and Interminable," 319.

115. Freud, "Analysis Terminable and Interminable," 320.

116. Again, we see this pattern repeatedly represented in science fiction, where the
very flawed human manages to overcome the dominant technological system which is
superior to us in seemingly every way.

117. Freud, "Analysis Terminable and Interminable," 321.

118. One of the selling points of Google's "Gmail" mail server is its large storage
capacity, which means that most users no longer have to *delete* any old messages. They
can be stored indefinitely.

119. Freud, "Analysis Terminable and Interminable," 317.

120. The most succinct example here would be the "millenium bug" that many believed would bring the entire industrialized world to an utter halt. At the time, not many
faulted the machines, but the failure of the human programmers to understand the signi-

ficance of not properly coding the switch from "99" to "00." Worst-case scenarios included total power shutdowns and accidental launches of ICBMs. A mistake in coding was potentially responsible for literally the end of the world.

Chapter Four

White Noise:
Jack Gladney and the
Evasion of Responsibility

The possibility that humans enframe the world technologically as a function of our biology sheds new light on posthumanism, particularly when we consider just how much of a role our own technological aspirations play in posthuman subjectivity. The self-awareness that drives posthumanism relies heavily on the liberal humanist subject as the one stable point of view from which we can discern our "selves" and the technological other.

Unfortunately, we come away from Lyotard and Freud schismatically, with the narrative and the technological vying for supremacy of the posthuman: we apprehend the information of the world technologically, but we "experience" and construct the world narratively. We aspire to technologically informed notions of completion, but settle for conclusions. The posthuman quest for compatibility becomes plagued by human feelings of inadequacy. Those feelings are based on our own human frailty and inability to process *our own* information.

Our suffering is two-fold: we are compelled by the inexhaustibility of the perceivable to keep uncovering information, but we are limited in our ability to use the information we uncover. The posthuman *knows* that it is composed of information, and it knows that the key to reaching its human potential lies in integrating itself into the "information" of the world without losing a cohesive self-image.

Subjectivity for the posthuman becomes dependent upon how effectively it can negotiate the boundary between the self and the technology through which that self is realized. The posthuman expresses its pain and suffering instrumentally, relying on technological artifacts to shoulder the burden of the human condition. We use the objects hoping that they will bring us relief, only to find that there is still more pain (physical, psychological, ontological) to be expressed.

Theorists such as Hayles and Haraway present us with scenarios of posthuman subjectivity that are achieved through a willing embrace of the technological. Being aware of the boundary between human self and technological other will make us more available to the possibility of transcendence that technology has to offer. We are composed of information, but the realities of biology make it impossible for us to access the full potential of that information. Through technology, posthumanism claims, we will be able to fully understand ourselves.[1]

Psychologically, the posthuman self aspires to a technologically informed model of humanity. It is a model unhindered by biological limitation, while still retaining the subjectivity unique to that very biology. It is a "datafied" self—one that is fully available to a complete integration with the information that composes the world, achieving the inside-out inversion that Scarry states is a way of making ourselves more available to the world. While this does not exactly represent a desire to upload the consciousness, this model still relies on the idea that it is possible to have a complete, datafied self somehow projected "out there," outside of the human body. It sees this model as a goal of completion. Achieving it will allow us to transcend the need for the technological supplement.

The "datafied" self we wish to see reflected in the system holds the promise of a perfect other to suffer with us, or *for* us. It is the other that is the perfect witness to our human suffering. It knows our pain, and it can simultaneously ease and eventually erase that pain. To be posthuman is to embrace technology so that it may embrace us. Ever-aware of its mortality, the posthuman seeks out the embrace with added urgency, before the human narrative comes to an end. Overshadowed by the impossibility of the embrace itself, we romanticize the quest, privileging the humanist subject by falling back on its imperfection. "I did the best I could, I am only human."

Heidegger and Lyotard both maintained that humans must take responsibility for their own relationships with technology. We must come to terms with the fact that we take in the world technologically (via a processing of information), but that the information we take in must *actively* be worked through via anamnesis, lest we be "pulled forward" by complexification. It is the human who is responsible for maintaining its agency in terms of the technological. Critical posthumanism, rather than centering our humanity on our human "responsibility" for taking in information technologically, sees complexification itself as our defining, human trait. Critical posthumanism also sees anamnesis as necessary for gaining the right relationship with technology, but as a means to an end, rather than as an ongoing process. A successful process of anamnesis also relies on an acknowledgment and eventual integration of the supplemental "other" (in psychoanalysis, the analyst). The posthuman has yet to do that; the technological other (whether manifested by information or artifact) is considered superior from the outset, and can never truly be integrated without losing our humanity.

Even though Oedipa Maas sought out an apparatus of interface to make contact with a superior technological other, she did so in an attempt to liberate herself from the Tristero. The difficulty with posthumanism is that it does not recognize how intrinsically linked technology and the human actually are. If we take in the world technologically, as Lyotard maintains, then the relationship posthumanism seeks out has always been present in each of us. Unfortunately, that relationship doesn't necessarily bring the transcendence the posthuman seeks.

Hayles's claim that we are already posthuman is based on the effects of our instrumental use of technology, *not* on the fact that our actual "taking in" of the world is technological. Without taking that into account, posthumanism views technology as a separate other to which we must bridge the gap so that we can become "fully" human. The boundary between human self and technological other becomes a defining one, where "extended embodied awareness" is delineated not by the body itself, but by the objects with which we expand our reach.

Therefore, the well-informed, hyper-but-critically-aware posthuman who aspires to full embodiment rearticulates its subjectivity in relation to the objects around it. Its sense of self relies on those objects to remain viable. Subjectivity, it would seem, takes the shape of its container. If we view technological objects and systems around us as ways to extend our embodied awareness, then a posthuman subjectivity is defined not by the body, but by the supplements we add to it. Its viability is directly dependent upon the material objects it uses. Scarry tells us that as human beings advance technologically, skill is "built into" the systems we create, and "built out" of the human him or herself. Taking posthuman subjectivity to its most extreme, one sees that the very ability to be self-aware becomes "outsourced" onto the objects around us. The "skill" of literally *being human* is "built out" of the human.

In this manner, the posthuman embrace becomes a submission to the technological other, rather than an assertion of the human. We initiate the embrace as a means of giving technology itself the permission to embrace us. Instead of "saving" us, the embrace becomes the human attempt to empower the technological other to define our boundaries for us. We submit our subjectivity to the technological other. And in so doing, we "give up" the responsibility of being human.

In Don DeLillo's *White Noise,* Jack Gladney represents just that kind of posthuman, and he provides us with the most contemporary example of posthuman subjectivity this far. Jack's attempts to become "aware" of the boundaries between himself and technology manifest themselves as an externalization of subjectivity. In the tradition of Scarry's belief that we constantly attempt to "turn ourselves inside out," Jack has essentially "outsourced" his subjectivity, becoming reliant upon technological/cultural artifacts to define him. When those artifacts fail him, he is faced with the reality of his narrative, and fears the conclusion he's being pulled toward. He refuses to accept this reality. Believing that he has no apparatus through which to mediate his narrative, he attempts to shift the blame for his situation on the very objects he empowered with his subjectivity in the first place. Jack attempts to evade the responsibility of his own humanity.

Authenticated and Confirmed:
Forgetting What Was Never Inscribed

> In the morning I walked to the bank. I went to the automated teller machine to check my balance. I inserted my card, entered my secret code, tapped out my request. The figure on the screen roughly corresponded to my independent estimates, feebly arrived at after long searches through documents, tormented arithmetic. Waves of relief and gratitude flowed over me. The system had blessed my life. I felt its support and approval. The system hardware, the mainframe sitting in a locked room in some distant city. What a pleasing interaction. I sensed that something of deep personal value, but not money, not that at all, had been authenticated and confirmed. A deranged person was escorted from the bank by two armed guards. The system was invisible, which made it all the more impressive, all the more disquieting to deal with. But we were in accord, at least for now. The networks, the circuits, the streams, the harmonies.[2]

Jack Gladney's faith in the system is established during his epiphany at the automated teller machine. Here, he performs a technological ritual of inclusion. The characterization of his code as "secret" establishes a special relationship between him and the system, giving him privileged status. This code, this information, belongs to him, and it is what defines him to the system. Here, some of posthumanism's most important assumptions are at work. Information is not only privileged as special, secret, and the key to his entry, but it is also treated as something solid that can be possessed.[3]

This becomes one of a number of moments when Jack submits to the superiority of the system. He admits that his own self generated information—the figures he had "feebly arrived" at—only "roughly" corresponded to the number on the screen. To Jack, it is the system's numbers (information) that are correct, rather than his own. Not once does he even consider the possibility that his numbers could be accurate and that the system's could be wrong. His own calculations were "tormented"—as if he were going through a sacred ordeal of initiation.

But just before Jack's inferiority manifests itself, he is the one in control: he is the one who initiated this contact in the first place. Even though he feels that he has been acknowledged by the machine, we cannot forget that the *feeling* he "receives" is a product of his own projection. The "blessing" erases that moment of initiation. Jack here is following the pattern of the sacred outlined in Scarry, first giving of himself and making himself available—*inserting* his card, *entering* his secret code—so that he may receive the blessing and acknowledgment of a system he believes to be superior.

Posthumanism misses this giving over and how that submission affects the individual's relationship to the technological other. For the posthuman, the giving over has always already been enacted. Neither Hayles nor Haraway discusses engaging the technological other as a *choice*. By not acknowledging that the human is *responsible* for initiating the technological embrace, the human becomes inferior from the outset. This is how the human—in Lyotard's terms—comes to be "pulled forward" by the instrumentality of technology. Indeed, we are all affected by technology whether or not we want to be, but posthuman subjectivity is dependent on this initial *consent* through which the system is first engaged. The choice must be made to invest the system with power so that it can invest us with power.

Note the change in tone as Jack sees his information projected on the screen: at first the figure on the screen only "roughly corresponds" to his "independent estimates," privileging him and his own abilities. It is *the system's* figures which "roughly correspond," *his estimates* which are "independent." But within that same sentence, the giving over takes place, and his once independent (quite possibly, superior) estimate is suddenly rendered feeble, and the product of "tormented" human endeavor. As soon as Jack has made this admission—or, more correctly, this *submission*—to the system, he becomes the recipient of relief. Although the relief originates from himself, he feels that it has been granted to him by the system. Jack gives over the responsibility of his own authentication to the system, rather than understanding that the feeling was self-generated. This moment represents the "initial trauma" that Lyotard outlines *The Inhuman*, and that Haraway discusses in her "Cyborg Manifesto." Jack initiated this contact. But it is erased by what he perceives as the system's blessing. This submission constitutes that which "could not have been forgotten because it was never inscribed."[4] It is this initial giving over that he later represses.

This blessing is the aspect of the "embrace" for which the posthuman lives. Jack's initial giving over of his code constitutes his reaching out to the machine. It is this first reaching out that invests the technological other with the power to acknowledge him. He empowers the system. In posthumanism, there is no recognition of the "giving over" that initiates the embrace. The posthuman, despite its initial feelings of inadequacy, always must make the first gesture toward the technological other in order for the embrace to be enacted. It must initiate the relationship, reaching out to the machine. This crucial, overlooked initial step invests the technological other with the power to initiate the embrace on its own. It is this step that becomes Lyotard's "initial trauma" that the posthuman represses.

For Jack, the agency that is "given over" during the embrace is represented as information. The privileging of information that is so central to posthumanism becomes the self-defining aspect of posthuman subjectivity. His information identifies him to the system, and allows the system to identify (and he thinks, *identify with*) him. The information is given over—and literally given up—to the system. After that, Jack's numbers no longer belonged to him, essentially relieving him of his responsibility for them. In so doing, they have been separated from his human endeavor. Relieved of their human burden, the numbers have been made *perfect* by the very act of giving over.

Once separated from him, this perfect data reside in a "mainframe sitting in a locked room in some [unnamed and unknown] distant city." Jack has become a truly *informed* posthuman. He does not look to upload his consciousness, nor does he wish to forgo his body. Instead, he has privileged the concept of information to such an extent that it has become "lifted out" of him. He values most highly his connection with his own, *disembodied, distant* information, and being in accord with it—even though it was always his to begin with. The posthuman does not seek out a better connection with technology; it seeks out a perfect connection with itself.

Jack has surrendered his responsibility for his information to the machine. The information is no longer his to have to deal with; it now belongs to the machine to keep and care for. This privileging of information also resonates with Heidegger's concept of *herausfordern*—the "setting in order" which characterizes life in the digital age. Yet in this case, the information which Jack is setting in order and privileging is his own. The numbers themselves can be viewed as information—a "standing reserve" that had to be "challenged forth." Jack has become blinded by the instrumentality of technology, illustrating Heidegger's and Lyotard's fears of placing too much importance on technological systems and artifacts. His life is so defined by instrumental views of technological systems that his own self-image is the product of a "setting-in-order." He further invests power in the system by viewing it as self regulating when he witnesses a "deranged person escorted from the bank by two armed guards." He views the guards as agents of the system. In Jack's eyes, not only can the system "confirm" and "authenticate," it can also *enforce* and *eject*. All the more reason for him to invest his faith in its power.

This is a sublime moment for Jack as he stands in awe at the power of the system. If his information is housed and protected within its confines, then he too shares in some of this power. In Oedipa Maas, we saw an individual who was suspicious of technological systems. Seeing iterations of herself scattered throughout the landscape of the Tristero, Oedipa sought a means of interface, perpetually putting off her "quest" until she could find one. What separates Oedipa from Jack Gladney is that she was looking for a way to take responsibility for the Tristero, but felt that she had no apparatus to do so. Although Oedipa never felt that she was in charge, she was still willing to make the attempt. Jack, on the other hand, has willingly given himself over to the system in exchange for its acknowledgment and protection.

The Sum of His Data:
Death in Not So Many Words

Jack's reliance on artifacts represents a continuation of Oedipa Maas's quest for an object of interface. However, in light of a more technologically complex (and complicated world), the desire for the apparatus has transformed itself. He is desperately attempting to achieve the inside out inversion that Scarry outlines.

The operative term here is "attempts." For Scarry, this inversion occurs when a specific object is created.

Similar to Heidegger's theories in "The Question Concerning Technology," Scarry believes that the creation and use of an object is the human's natural and effective expression of suffering. But in light of a perceived superior system (e.g., religion, technology), the human can merely attempt—rather than achieve—this inversion. The "other" which we attempt to make ourselves available to is actually a product of our own projection, via the process of analogical verification. The use of technology in such situations becomes a manifestation of faith—the desire to give ourselves over to a system which we believe is superior. The artifacts around Jack define him because he *believes* they define him, because he has already invested them with that power. In so doing, he has actually repressed the initial empowering.

Jack Gladney's subjectivity has been expressed and externalized to the world around him to such an extent that he is unwilling and unable to realize that he initiated that very expression. As critic Leonard Wilcox states, Jack's dependence on the artifacts of a technological culture points to an emergence of a new form of subjectivity characterized by an inability to construct an image of oneself separate from the world he or she inhabits.[5] The parameters of his "self" are defined by the technological artifacts (and commodified culture) around him. This serves him well, and becomes an easy way to navigate through the postmodern world he inhabits. He doesn't have to worry about "substance" as long as the objects which define him remain in place.

Jack Gladney knowingly experiences joy at consumer mantras that emanate from his television set. He even "worships" at the supermarket, which becomes the main cultural center of Blacksmith.[6] Jack experiences pleasure when he understands the irony of (not) seeing the "most photographed barn in America,"[7] or hearing his daughters repeat names of products ("Toyota Celica") in their sleep.[8] This is consistent with the posthuman who is making him or herself "available" to the world. He knowingly acknowledges the fact that his joys in life are instrumental, and they are firmly rooted in consumer culture. He allows the outer trappings of his life define who he is.

Although Jack considers himself first and foremost a college professor, his credentials are firmly rooted in his professorial trappings. When, early in his career, the college chancellor warned him against making a "feeble presentation of self,"[9] Jack attempted to fill himself out by augmenting his appearance rather than solidifying his scholarship. He donned heavy glasses and renamed himself "J. A. K.," a name which, to his wife, "intimated dignity, significance, and prestige." Despite this, even though he is chair of Hitler Studies, he cannot speak German. But Jack fails to escape his insecurity. His technological faith wavers, as he admits that he is the "false character that follows the name around."[10] To combat that insecurity, he simply attacks it instrumentally, trying to shore himself up with more "things."

In posthuman fashion, Jack views information as something that has substance, and conversely, views anything with substance as a manifestation of information. Information is simply another *thing* which can help flesh him out. His subjectivity is maintained by his faith that his essence (as data) remains safely distant and protected—to be called upon when needed to "back him up." Similar to Haraway's cyborg, Jack believes the information that composes him is beyond reproach, and immune to the imperfections and limitations of biology—including death itself. His information is ethereal, clean, and perfect. The difference between Jack and Haraway's cyborg is that the former has externalized this information. Although he *is* his data, he envisions his "true" data to be outside of himself, housed in some far distant databank. It somehow seems safer there than it ever could be in his physical body. Jack privileges his information over his physicality.

Jack finds, however, that his "datafied" self is just as susceptible to death as his physical self. When a freight train carrying chemicals crashes close to Blacksmith, the Gladney family must evacuate. Relying heavily on his faith in the objects that define him, and on his own hubris that his information will remain protected, Jack refuses to believe that he is susceptible to any kind of danger. He continually questions the logic of evacuation, specifically because he is a "college professor," and that one doesn't see "a college professor rowing a boat down his own street in one of those TV floods."[11] On his way to a shelter, even as the airborne toxic event looms overhead releasing contaminated snow, Jack decides to pull over and refuel his car. He is aware of the danger (it has been broadcast on the radio *and* repeated to him by his son, Heinrich), but he still allows himself to be exposed to the contaminated snow.

Jack's decision to leave the car and allow himself to be exposed is an iteration of the initial submission he made to the ATM. However, in this instance, Jack is relying on his faith in the objects around him (his very expressed identity as a college professor/father/provider) to protect him from harm. He is not thinking of his human vulnerability as much as he is thinking of his posthuman invulnerability. His data will always remain intact, especially since it is so far away.

The five minutes that Jack was exposed, however, was enough to create a "situation." Although he did not feel any ill effects, when he arrives at a shelter, a SIMUVAC[12] official explains that Jack's exposure had caused some anomalous readings in his data. When Jack asks him whether or not he will die, the official responds cryptically "Not as such" and "Not in so many words."[13] Regarding Jack's "situation," the SIMUVAC official explains:

> I didn't say it. The computer did. The whole system says it. It's what we call a massive database tally. Gladney, J. A. K. I punch in the name, the substance, the exposure time and then I tap into your computer history. Your genetics, your personals, your medicals, your psychologicals, your police-and-hospitals. It comes back pulsing stars. This doesn't mean anything is going to happen to you as such, at least not today or tomorrow. It just means that you are the sum total of your data. No man escapes that.[14]

The "pulsing stars" and "bracketed numbers" are unreadable to Jack, but they suggest that his exposure to Nyodene D has brought his mortality to the fore-front. Death has entered his data. The data that Jack thought was protected, dis-tanced, and immune from any threat had suddenly been corrupted by an airborne toxic event that touched Jack directly. His information was not as sacred as he believed it to be, destabilizing what had become his entire posthuman belief system. From this point on, Jack's "objectified subjectivity" is thrown into disar-ray. He no longer feels the same sense of comfort or awe that once sustained him.

Ironically, the fact that Jack's inevitable death is represented in his code il-lustrates an aspect of the posthuman dream: his full human embodiment—mortality and all—is *perfectly* reflected in his data. He is the sum of his informa-tion. But this is not at all what Jack (or the posthuman) actually *wants* from his data. The posthuman is not looking for a perfect *reflection*. It is looking for a perfect *supplement*. Jack looks to his data as the information that can fill in the hole that death has placed in his being:

> I think I felt as if a doctor had held and X-ray to the light showing a star-shaped hole in the center of one of my vital organs. Death has entered. It is inside you. You are said to be dying yet are separate from the dying. . . . It is when death is rendered graphically, is televised so to speak, that you sense and eerie separa-tion between your condition and yourself. A network of symbols has been in-troduced, an entire awesome technology wrested from the gods. It makes you feel like a stranger in your own dying.[13]

Jack believes he is dying because death has entered his information, not be-cause he is feeling any physical symptoms. He never acknowledges the fact that he himself allowed it to enter. Since he considers information as sacred, the fact that it could somehow be susceptible makes it more terrifying to him than if he felt that "star-shaped hole" in his own internal organs. He wants his information to fill in the gaps in his being—to be the supplement that will complete his in-complete, flawed, and very mortal self. A system that embraces him should also protect him, and, most importantly, *complete* him.

The introduction of death into his information has also had the unsettling ef-fect of highlighting Jack's outsourced subjectivity. He feels "separated" from himself, and cannot come to terms with his mortality. It becomes apparent that the comfort he felt when interacting with the "system" was rooted in its optional, supplemental nature. That is to say, he achieved "pleasing interactions" when it suited him and when he needed authentication. He achieved that when he sought those interactions out on his own terms and when he initiated the submission himself. Although he was aware even during his ATM epiphany that the system could reject him, his current frustration stems from the fact that he hasn't been *rejected* at all. Both he and his information are totally in accord. The connection is still there. Jack is being perfectly reflected, rather than perfectly supple-mented. In his view, his submission to the system should have relieved him of responsibility for his information. Even if his body was exposed, his information should have remained untouched.

Although it never implies that our information will make us invulnerable, posthumanism fosters this belief by elevating the role of information itself. If we can take control of our information—if we can take control of the means of inscription of our data—then we can achieve our full potential. The subtext is that our human potential is dependent on the right supplements to our human bodies, and that those supplements will give us abilities that we do not currently possess, or will augment those abilities to such an extent that we will become "better" humans. There is an implied promise that having access to all of our information, being able to make all of it available, will help us transcend the very parameters of our humanity.

For Jack, this promise is shattered by the fact that he *literally* has possession of his code. As the novel progresses, numerous tests, hospital visits, and consultations have produced an envelope filled with read-outs, reports, images, test results, etc. He *makes no attempt* to read any of the information it contains. Even taking into account the possibility that the information may be "in code" and unreadable to someone without a medical background, Jack avoids seeing his doctor, Dr. Chakravaty, and instead hides the information in his desk drawer. Jack has invested so much power in his information that he is scared of it. He refuses to take responsibility for it, just as he consistently refuses to take responsibility for exposing himself the airborne toxic event in the first place. He allows himself to be victimized by technology.

Jack has been inscribed in the system, illustrating an aspect of Haraway's cyborg nightmare where technology is used against a person's wishes to render that individual into code. Haraway's cyborg dream represents the struggle to gain control of the means of inscription. Jack, on the other hand, has given up the struggle. He has willingly embraced technology, and has willingly been embraced by it. But it has not brought him the protection he wanted. He has not gained the completion he needs to transcend his own human frailties. Jack's "cyborg self" is (rightfully) as mortal as he is.

The fact that Jack's data is susceptible to death destabilizes his posthuman subjectivity. Like the believer who falls into apostasy, he finds the icons of worship useless, and the rituals of their use, meaningless. The objects on which he relied to define him and maintain his posthuman subjectivity have suddenly lost their power to affirm him. After the airborne toxic event, Jack no longer feels any sense of authentication or even comfort in the technological and cultural artifacts with which he has surrounded himself. On the contrary, he feels that they are encroaching upon him, and blocking his attempts to make sense of what happened. From a posthumanist perspective, Jack is in need of anamnesis. However, it is his very posthuman subjectivity which precludes any kind of anamnesis. He does not know *how* to engage events in a non-instrumental way.

It is important to keep in mind that although Jack no longer feels "authenticated" by the objects around him, that does not mean that he no longer feels a connection with them. He continues to empower them. But now they have become impediments. His connection to them has been transformed into a connection to mortality itself. Rather than take control of the situation directly (by bringing the information contained in his test results to his doctor for interpretation), Jack instead looks for something else to blame. He feels out of control, but blames that feeling on the material objects around him, and begins a series of purges to uncomplicate his life. Even though he is purging things, it is still a manifestation of the Heideggerian "setting in order." And Jack, still the consummate posthuman, once again submits to the artifacts around them by subconsciously granting them power and "immensity":

> The more things I threw away, the more I found. The house was a maze of old and tired things. There was an immensity of things, an overburdening weight, a connection, a mortality. I stalked the rooms, flinging things into cardboard boxes. . . . No one helped me. I didn't want help or company or human understanding.[16]

The objects that once gave Jack comfort now highlight his isolation and weakness. He is truly suffering here—not from his disease—but from his continuing refusal to take responsibility for his situation, and, ultimately, his own identity. The "things" around him are the physical expressions of himself, but they give him no comfort. He is "connected" to them, but that connection brings no relief. The purges become more personal, as he begins to throw away his old research papers, academic awards, and degrees. All of these are manifestations of complexification itself, and his interaction with them soon degenerate into the "barbarism" that Lyotard believes characterizes our current techno-scientific means of taking in the world.[17] His final purge becomes more primal and public as he picks through more intimate aspects of his life in front of his two daughters:

> I was in a vengeful and near savage state. I bore a personal grudge against these things. *Somehow, they'd put me in this fix.* They'd dragged me down, made escape impossible. The two girls followed me around, observing a respectful silence. . . . I threw away diplomas, certificates, awards and citations. When the girls stopped me, I was working the bathrooms, discarding used bars of soap, damp towels, shampoo bottles with streaked labels and missing caps.[18]

Jack's helplessness is compounded as he is further "exposed." He cannot discern any value in the things he purges, and what should be his most prized professional trappings (his diplomas, certificates, etc.) are lumped together with discarded soap and shampoo bottles. He has put the responsibility for his situation on the objects around him rather than himself.

We return again to Lyotard's concept of complexification: Jack's motive drive has always been development; he has been creating and recreating himself recursively by adding layers of "stuff." His ontology has always been information; he believed that the possibility for a perfected "being" could be found only in his disembodied data. His logic has always been complexification; the more things he collected, the more possibility for answers and advancement. He also relied on his faith in the "inexhaustibility of the perceivable"—that in any information uncovered, he might find the "answers" to his problem. But as we have already witnessed, Jack literally holds his information but gains no answers from it.

Do Not Advance:
Resisting the Conclusion

The airborne toxic event could easily be classified as a trauma for Jack, but it is not the *originary* trauma that is causing his current suffering. After exposure, he feels as if his consent to being represented by technology has been taken away from him, even though he willingly gave up that consent prior to the accident. He feels separated from his information, but the separation comes from his own unwillingness to engage that information. Although he no longer feels a sense of satisfaction from the objects around him, he still grants them power—only he does so without wanting to. The artifacts of commodified culture were the tools through which Jack made meaning. When they were his to control (or when he gave them permission to control him), he could easily negotiate his way through his technified world.

Before the accident, even death itself was easily "catagorized" and "classified" according to a technological model. Earlier in the novel, when he is contemplating his relationship with his wife, Babette, Jack admits to his ongoing preoccupation:

> Who will die first?
>   The question comes up from time to time, like where are the car keys. It ends a sentence, prolongs a glance between us. I wonder if the thought itself is part of the nature of physical love, a reverse Darwinism that awards sadness and fear to the survivor. Or is it some inert element in the air we breathe, a rare thing like neon, with a melting point, an atomic weight?[19]

Jack can deal with death as long as it remains an "inert element." At this point, it had not yet been "activated" by the airborne toxic event. His faith in technology helped him to keep death at bay by thinking about it in scientific terms. Jack's approach of seeing *all things* as a manifestation of information is based on the posthuman assumption that information can travel seamlessly from one substrate to another. This "commutability of signs" allows death itself to be simulated and represented in such a way that "the experience of dying is utterly mediated by technology and eclipsed by a world of the symbolic."[20] As long as Jack *can* mediate death through technological metaphors, it remains at a safe distance from him.

But with that relationship destabilized, all of those objects suddenly got in the way of his ability to make sense of, or to *work through*, the reality of his mortality. After the airborne toxic event, Jack attempts to engage in some form of anamnesis, but he has no *apparatus* through which to perform such an anamnesis. He repeatedly tries to re-position himself to gain a better vantage-point in relation to his situation. Here, the difficulty of a posthuman application of anamnesis becomes apparent.

Successful anamnesis, according to Lyotard, requires the individual to take responsibility for the information he or she is taking in technologically. It must be actively worked through in an ongoing manner. Jack takes responsibility for his information only superficially. He "possesses it" but refuses to engage it. He is afraid of it because he is working under the posthuman assumption that his information (and the technology that uncovered it, and that he needs to decipher it) has power over him. Thus, Jack, as a posthuman, is trying to engage his information after he's already submitted to it. In order to work through his information successfully, he must take responsibility for it by acknowledging his own submission to (and subsequent empowering of) the system.

Posthumanism as a discourse goes into the process of anamnesis already assuming the insurmountable superiority of the technological other without understanding its submission to it, thus circumventing the anamnetic process itself. No transference is possible. The posthuman—like Jack—centers its "humanity" in the process of complexification (the uncovering of information) itself, rather than in the human ability to make sense of complexification through narrative. When the tools of interpretation are rendered ineffective, then interpretation becomes impossible.

Posthumanism—even critical posthumanism—invests the very ability to "work though" information and experience in the instrumentality of technology. Our ability to decode information is as good only as the apparatus through which we take it in. It cannot work though its originary trauma because it identifies that trauma in the wrong place: posthumanism sees it as occurring some time *after* the embrace has taken place, rather than seeing it as the initiating of the embrace itself.

Furthermore, posthumanism views anamnesis as a means to an end, a task that can be completed, thus completing the human. But this means to an "end," this movement toward conclusion, is exactly what Jack fears the most. To Jack, narrative (especially as characterized as narrative "plots") represents an inevitable movement toward death. Before the airborne toxic event, he is most frightened by death when it functions *narratively*, as the conclusion of a plot. Even before his exposure, an uninvited, narrative introduction of death causes a very anxious response:

> When the showing ended, someone asked about the plot to kill Hitler. The discussion moved to plots in general. I found myself saying to the assembled heads, "All plots tend to move deathward. This is the nature of plots. Political plots, terrorist plots, lovers' plots, narrative plots, plots that are part of children's games. We edge nearer death every time we plot. It is like a contract that all must sign, the plotters as well as those who are the targets of the plot."
> Is this true? Why did I say it? What does it mean?[21]

Jack's fear of death has always been a part of him, and his expressed subjectivity is a result of that fear. Every object that he possesses, and that he empowers to represent him, is also a manifestation of his fear of death. Each object becomes another layer that keeps him distanced from what death represents. Each becomes another "complication" that keeps him woven into a larger, technified system of culture. Jack believes that the more deeply he is implicated in that culture, the more difficult it is for "death" to take him. He has dispersed himself.

If death comes to claim him, he must be "put together" first. This is why narrative—what he characterizes as "plots"—is so threatening to him. Any plot in which he's implicated threatens to integrate him, and this make visible the gaps in his identity. As Jack's plot progresses deathward, "the narrative development itself interrelates . . . relations of knowledge and power," bringing the disparate aspects of his life into a relationship that illustrates exactly how superficial those various aspects of his life actually were.[22]

If Jack's subjectivity is posthuman, and he has used the objects around him to "scatter" that subjectivity, a narrative plot is something that could possibly *unify* him, bringing all the disparate aspects of his personality together into one unified whole whose weaknesses, frailties, and flaws are apparent to the outside world.[23] Jack, as a posthuman, aspires to completion. The narrative plot, by bringing all of his "pieces together," threatens to complete him without his consent. After the airborne toxic event, *all* of Jack's cultural roles and social identities are pulled back together as "the sum total of his data," and are rendered completely ineffective as a remedy to the death that was already present in his life. Now that death has entered, by his own logic, he has been implicated in a plot. Unfortunately, there is no "apparatus" through which he can read it.

The very same technological metaphors that were used to keep death at bay have become the means by which Jack empowers death. One would think that completion would be something desirable for him. He aspires to completion, but he does so instrumentally. Before the airborne toxic even, he believed that his data would save him, and be the supplement that fills in his "gaps." Completion becomes a means to an end. It is not death that Jack fears; it is what death represents: conclusion.

After dropping off one of his daughters at the airport, Jack takes an unexplained detour to the local cemetery. "Beyond the traffic noise," he "remained in one spot, waiting to feel the peace that is supposed to descend upon the dead."[24] Again, he projects an internal emotion/feeling outward, and waits for the experience to be bestowed upon him, rather than be the one generating the experience itself. And again, he equates "power" with a technological metaphor of energy. The dead, it would seem, are also part of a system:

> The power of the dead is that we think they see us all the time. The dead have a presence. Is there a level of energy based solely on the dead? They are also in the ground, of course, asleep and crumbling. Perhaps we are what they dream.
>
> May the days be aimless. Let the seasons drift. Do not advance the action according to a plan.[25]

Jack believes that the power of the dead lies in their ability to see everyone, all of the time—unifying experience in their gaze. To be the dream of the dead is to be enclosed and encompassed within a closed system. But, since the dead are *always* dead, the dream continues, endlessly. It is this aimless endlessness which Jack, and the posthuman, desires. Here, he performs a somewhat misleading "prayer to the system" that is similar to Oedipa's "prayer" to the Nefastis machine.

Although it may seem that he is praying to a non-technological system, Jack is, in fact, praying to what he perceives as a system which is even larger than the one represented by the ATM. What Jack is praying *for* is a subversion of an end. If a narrative plot always leads to death, then a drifting aimlessness represents an existence which can remain indefinitely. Unlike Oedipa, Jack does not need the system to "show itself," nor does he need to know that he is implicated in it; his posthuman subjectivity is proof that he knows that. Instead, he does not wish to advance. He wants *no progress*. A narrative will fill him in, complete him, and in his own mind, conclude him.[26]

This may appear completely antithetical to posthumanism, which *seems* to want a progression from the limited biological human to a post-human who has achieved full embodied awareness. However, the posthuman knows that this awareness is an impossibility. It *constantly strives for it, but does not achieve it,* thus, indefinitely postponing the full realization of posthumanism itself. For what purpose? Ultimately, as a way to privilege the limited, frail, weak *human.* Posthumanism becomes a more "informed" way to retain the liberal humanist subject while simultaneously rejecting it. In this manner, we remain human in light of dehumanizing, and at times, inhuman technological system. It also turns the failure itself into a mark of human resolve and tenacity.

Posthumanism also becomes a way to evade responsibility for *being* human, and taking control of the systems of power which the it has characterized (especially in Haraway) as being the tools which have oppressed us. The liberal humanist subjects remains in tact. Both Lyotard and Heidegger understood this, and it is why each espouses a form of "responsibility" to come to terms with the essence of technology as an aspect of ourselves, rather than as a technified other that we can use to evade the realities of our human existence. With the idea that there is always more to be uncovered, we gain the ability to keep going on without having to actually come to a "conclusion." We are also given something to blame if we fail, and something to distract us so that we can hide our own lack of ability and desire to take responsibility.

While a posthuman outsourcing of subjectivity may give us comfort now, its practical and theoretical implications reach far beyond the ontological "flailing about" of Jack Gladney. It leads to a dependence on a romanticized fantasy of what technology actually does for us, rather than a concentration on what we can do with technology. By losing track of who initiated the "embrace" between human and technological other, we are placed at the mercy of the very feelings of inadequacy and "incompleteness" that we seek to assuage. If posthumanism sees itself as a way to navigate us through our technological development, then it must come to terms with our relationship to technology at the moment when we reach for it in the first place.

Jack Gladney showed us the implications of posthuman subjectivity, specifically through his willingness to blindly hand over "consent" to the technological other. He relied on instrumental manifestations of technology to define himself, and found that he was unprepared to engage his narrative. His empowering of the systems and objects around him allowed him to place the blame for his own mortality on technology. Individually, Jack made his choice to submit to the system, but could not come to terms with the implications of that choice, primarily because the "giving over" he enacted erased the act itself. Posthuman subjectivity is contingent upon this forgetting.

Notes

1. I purposely use the qualifier "fully" here. Although an argument can be made that it is impossible to "fully" understand anything, the posthuman dream relies on a full and total understanding of self through technology.

2. Don DeLillo, *White Noise* (New York: Penguin Books, 1986), 46.

3. Interestingly, this code was initially given to Jack by the system itself. We are always given a "personal identification number" or "PIN" by our various financial institutions. Although sometimes we have the option to change that PIN, the option itself depends upon having the initial PIN in the first place.

4. Lyotard, *Inhuman*, 54.

5. Leonard Wilcox, "Baudrillard, DeLillo's *White Noise*, and the Discourse of the Posthuman," *Contemporary Literature* 32.3 (1991), 347-8. Wilcox here relies heavily on the Baudrillardian concept of "the end of interiority." See Jean Baudrillard "The Ecstasy of Communication," in *The Anti-Aesthetic: Essay on Postmodern Culture,* ed. Hal Foster (Port Townsend, WA: Bay, 1983), 126-34.

6. "The high temple of this society, the point where forces converge and data are coded most intensely, is the supermarket. It provides the setting for contested meanings that may or may not inhere in the text's noise." N. Katherine Hayles, "Postmodern Parataxis: Embodied Texts, Weightless Information," *American Literary History* 2.3 (1990), 208.

7. When Jack visits the barn with his colleague, Murray Siskind, he stands in silent agreement with his friend's assessment of the situation: "Being here is a kind of spiritual surrender. We see only what others see. The thousands who were here in the past, those who will come in the future. We've agreed to be part of a collective perception. This literally colors our vision. A religious experience in a way, like all tourism." DeLillo, *White Noise*, 12.

8. "Toyota Celica. . . . A long moment passed before I realized this was the name of an automobile. The truth only amazed me more. The utterance was beautiful and mysterious, gold-shot with looming wonder. It was like the name of an ancient power in the sky, tablet-carved in cuneiform. It made me feel that something hovered. But how could this be? A simple brand name. An ordinary car. How could these near-nonsense words, murmured in a child's restless sleep, make me sense a meaning, a presence? She was

only repeating some TV voice. Toyota Corolla, Toyota Celica, Toyota Cressida. Supranational names, computer-generated, more or less universally pronounceable . . . Whatever its source, the utterance struck me with the impact of a moment of splendid transcendence." DeLillo, *White Noise*, 155.

9. DeLillo, *White Noise*, 17.

10. DeLillo, *White Noise*, 17.

11. DeLillo, *White Noise*, 114.

12. Acronym for "SIMulated eVACuation."

13. DeLillo, *White Noise*, 140.

14. DeLillo, *White Noise*, 141.

15. DeLillo, *White Noise*, 141-42.

16. DeLillo, *White Noise*, 262.

17. Lyotard, *Inhuman*, 62.

18. DeLillo, *White Noise*, 294 (emphasis mine).

19. DeLillo, *White Noise*, 15.

20. Wilcox, "Discourse of the Posthuman," 352.

21. DeLillo, *White Noise*, 26.

22. Marie Christine Leps, "Empowerment Through Information: A Discursive Critique," *Cultural Critique* 31 (1995), 192.

23. Each aspect of Jack's personality contains its own series of "gaps." He is a husband (even though this is currently his third marriage). He is a father (even though he does not have a "normal" relationship with any of his children). He is a professor (who is only an "expert" in a field *he* created—"Hitler Studies," and who doesn't speak German).

24. DeLillo, *White Noise*, 97.

25. DeLillo, *White Noise*, 98.

26. Jack's own conclusion in *White Noise* is marked once again by his instrumental view of completion. When viewed in terms of a "plot," after Jack realizes that Babette has been taking Dylar, a drug that erases her fear of death, and that she obtained the drug by sleeping with its creator, Willie Mink, Jack's new-found goal is to confront (and kill) Mink. Even though it seemed as if Jack was taking the situation into his own hands by *forcing* a conclusion with Mink's death, Jack did so by trying to place *his own death* onto someone else. Temporarily alienated from the artifacts that defined him, he attempts to project his mortality onto someone else. Again, this is not so much a desire to overcome death as it is to evade it. In posthuman fashion, he gives death itself a quantitative value, and views it as something with substance that can be "traded" or "passed along" from person to person, or from person to object.

Conclusion

A.I. Artificial Intelligence:
Accepting Obsolescence

I submit a concluding image of posthuman suffering, as a means to illustrate more directly the theoretical "choreography" of the posthuman embrace. In the 2002 film *A.I.: Artificial Intelligence*, the Swinton family faces the ultimate implication of that embrace, and the audience is exposed to the possibility of humanity handing over its "skill"—or capacity for narrative—to the machine. I believe that the film presents a disturbing scenario which could potentially become part of a larger, posthuman mythology: That humanity's extinction is imminent, but that we will remain "alive" as the memories of our machines. Posthumanism has established the parameters for this mythology by privileging information to such an extent that humanity itself is characterized collectively as a pattern of information.

The film presents a world already ravaged by global warming (all coastal cities have been destroyed), overpopulation (families in industrial nations must be licensed to have children), and dehumanization (most menial tasks are handled by androids, called "mechas"). The Swinton family's only son has been stricken with a disease which medicine cannot yet cure. The boy is held in cryogenic stasis, while his parents are held in their own state of reserve, not knowing whether to grieve or hope. Doctors tell them their son is "merely pending."

The fragility of the Swintons' son represents the fragility of the future of the human race. Martin *may* be saved, but only by technological advancement. It is not a question of whether or not technology can save him; instead, it is a question of whether or not his parents can survive long enough to see that day come. From the outset, humanity in *A.I.* is on the wane. Biological physicality betrays humans on multiple levels. A "natural death" for Martin is held in reserve, and Monica, his mother, is most sensitive to her son's "pending" status: she does not know whether to mourn or hope. In Martin's doctor's words, however, "medicine tells us that mourning is inappropriate."

Martin and his family reside in that "middle state" which characterizes posthumanism. The posthuman does not specifically avoid the future; instead, it avoids taking responsibility for it. Neither Monica nor Henry can "pull the plug" on their son, because technology promises them that a cure will be found. The responsibility for his future is literally out of their hands, but they have not realized that *they* are the ones who have handed it over.[1]

123

In another posthuman maneuver, the Swintons do make an attempt to bring an end to their own suffering (and avoid responsibility for the future) by *imposing* a conclusion, which they hope will complete them as a family. Monica and Henry turn to a technological savior, David, to replace their son. David is an advanced mecha who, in the words of his creator, Dr. Richard Hobby, is programmed to "love like the love of a child for its parents. . . . A robot child who will genuinely love the parent or parents it imprints on, with a love that will never end." Furthermore, this mecha is built with "a mind," in which "an inner world of metaphor, of intuition, of self-motivated reasoning" will be created through his ability to love.

In this case, the fundamental human skill of utilizing metaphor, making meaning, and creating narrative is outsourced to David. He has been given the ultimate human quality: the ability to create a narrative—a narrative predicated on *love*. The difficulty that arises, however, is that the narrative (and ensuing love) from which David operates is not human. Lyotard implies that narrative is a way for humans to make sense of information temporally, in light of our own limited memories and ultimate mortality. David, however, can remember everything ever said to him, and is immortal. David possesses the ability to create a "perfect" narrative that does not have death as its conclusion or motivating force. He stands to take what is the most unique characteristic of humanity and perfect it. He also can grant an unconditional love that is not limited by mortality. The only problem is that he expects an impossible unconditional love in return.[2]

In *A.I.,* humanity has achieved the unspoken posthuman dream of creating a perfect other that fills in the spaces of human imperfection. David's arrival potentially "fills in" and completes the Swinton family. He stands to be a perfect child who never ages, and would become a perfect acknowledgement of the Swintons' identity as parents. The film also fulfills another unspoken posthuman dream: that imperfect humanity can indeed create perfection. Like a Christ-figure, David is fully human in his need to create a narrative (he needs to be loved, and needs to be needed), but fully "divine" in the perfection of that narrative (he cannot forget anything). And like a Christ-figure, David ultimately shoulders humanity's sins, and "redeems" us by carrying the collective human narrative beyond the boundaries of death, and human extinction. But for this to happen, David first had to be empowered to do so; he needed to be embraced.

The Imprinting Protocol:
The Posthuman Embrace Revealed

When Henry first brings David home, Monica is "freaked out" by him because he looks "too real." Although David is an advanced mecha, he invites interaction just as any technological system does. He is following the letter of his programming, "inserting himself" into family interactions in order to gain attention (in an attempt to convince Monica to "imprint" on him). When Monica is alone, David is always present. She tries to ignore him at first, but he watches and mimics her behavior and, not unlike toys today that use rudimentary artificial intelligence, he *learns*. At first, the Swintons never seem comfortable around David, but they awkwardly learn to live with him. David is a discomforting reminder of the family's own "incomplete" and/or "pending" nature. That is, until David shows a glimmer of humanity. At the dining room table, when Monica attempts to slurp a strand of pasta into her mouth, David points and laughs.

At this moment, David is mimicking a human trait that puts him—momentarily—in a superior position. He is not laughing *with* Monica, he seems to be laughing *at* her. To the Swintons, he seems to understand that what has happened to Monica is "silly" and potentially embarrassing, thus playing on human vanity. After he laughs at her, both Henry and Monica also laugh, thus reinforcing his own behavior; which is actually reinforcing *their* belief that he is finding humor in the situation. The tension is broken. And in this quick moment of mimicry, David gains enough trust from Monica for her to consider performing the "imprinting protocol" where David's "love" is activated.

In terms of posthumanism, this initial "reaching out" of David explains how humans can convince themselves—often subconsciously—of the superiority of the technological other. At first, David is a creepy nuisance. He is an intrusion into Monica's private life.[3] But his constant attempts to attract attention are merely a set of programmed behaviors designed to encourage human interaction. It is Monica's own lack which makes her sensitive to David's advances. An inability to reach a conclusion regarding her biological child makes David's permanence attractive. Although David's laughter at the dinner table was forced and very "artificial," Monica interprets it as a human response. Furthermore, she sees his laughter as a "reaching out." In her weakened emotional state, Monica projects her own human loneliness onto David, and feels obliged to go ahead with the procedure.

The imprinting procedure itself is primarily based on language and code. There are a series of words that must be spoken in the correct order so that David's love can be "activated." David's initial query, asking Monica if they're playing a game, causes Monica to respond awkwardly; both verbally (via constant pauses and "uhs"), and physically (she must reach around to the back of his neck to properly make contact. Although the protocol procedure is primarily verbal, there is a very significant physical component involved.

Before the imprinting begins, Monica, with the directions for imprinting in one hand, *kneels* in a submissive position before a seated David. With both figures in profile, David is seated *above* Monica, in a dominant position. All of Monica's subsequent questions and directions need to be "offered up" to David. Similar to Jack Gladney's interaction with the ATM, and Oedipa Maas' interaction with the Nefastis machine, Monica has already set herself up as inferior to David even though she is the one initiating the protocol. She also receives affirmation from him when she asks if he understands. This is a purely posthuman tableau: an incomplete, wounded, and suffering human looks up to a technological system for acknowledgment and affirmation, empowering it to do so. Even if Monica believes David to be inferior, it is only because she herself as not having given him the proper "code" to be activated. The reason he has been so "creepy" and awkward is not *his fault*, but the Swinton family's. Although one can say that she is now "taking responsibility" for David, she is doing so *after his superiority has already been, albeit subconsciously, acknowledged.* The procedure only continues after *David* gives Monica his permission. In posthuman terms, Monica always views David as superior in some form. She does not understand how he works, but as technology, David holds the promise of some kind of acknowledgment and completion. The possibility of him assuming the role of her son is contingent upon Monica making herself available to him via the imprinting protocol.

Immediately after he affirms that he can pay attention to Monica's directions and listen to the words she is about to speak, Monica *reaches up* to David's neck, then places her fingers on the back of his neck in a somewhat awkward, initial embrace (similar to Jack's "punching in of his code" to the ATM).

Whether we consider David to be a manifestation of Hayles's posthuman or Haraway's Cyborg, both possibilities are predicated on human insecurity. Every time we reach out to technological systems, we are doing so to satisfy a need, or to compensate for a perceived inability or limitation. So often, the reaching out to the technological other is "one handed," as we hold onto the "procedure," or a manifestation of the physical boundary between ourselves and the machine. Posthumanism is aware of the boundary as long as "one hand" remains on the procedural side of the interface. But the problem arises when our own desire causes us to "let go." Oedipa Maas could not *see* the Nefastis machine acknowledge her, because she followed the "procedures" of contact to the letter. She did not have the luxury of the direct acknowledgement which David gives Monica. Jack Gladney does let go, but the embrace he sought was more abstract. The reaching out is again affirmed by David. Monica then momentarily asserts her authority, but somewhat tentatively, asking David if her contact is hurting him. David responds that it does not.

Monica then must complete the rest of the imprinting protocol by speaking a series of words, while simultaneously looking directly into David's eyes. Although she cannot maintain the gaze continuously (she breaks it to read the words), she *speaks* the words while looking at him. David is still in a superior position, while Monica's hand remains on the back of David's neck. There is a noticeable awkwardness, however, in her attempt to do both at the same time. The posthuman also retains this awkwardness; the awareness of the boundary is difficult to maintain, but we straddle both worlds as best as we humanly can. She continues, again, tentatively:

> MONICA: Okay. Now. Look at me? Ready? Cirrus. Socrates. Particle. Decibel. Hurricane. Dolphin. Tulip. Monica. David. Monica. . . . All right. . . . I wonder if I did that right? I don't . . .

At the moment Monica questions her own human ability to perform the imprinting procedure (and re-directs her gaze to the instruction card), an imprinted, and visibly altered David intervenes and indirectly reassures her by asking her what the words were for, calling her—for the first time—"Mommy."[4]

At the moment the word "Mommy" is uttered, Monica looks away from the written procedures and looks pleadingly into David's eyes, stunned, asking, "What did you call me?" David repeats his response, only to have Monica ask him once again, "Who am I, David?" Before he verbally answers her question, David *reaches downward toward the kneeling Monica*, as if in heavenly visitation. As he does so, she drops the instructions to her side—effectively discarding—or forgetting—the initial imprinting procedures. David's "reaching out" to her is a manifestation of the authenticating and confirming aspects that Jack Gladney experiences at the ATM, and basically erases the evidence of the initial imprinting itself. As our technological systems become more complex the procedures of their use (the skill needed to engage them) become easier to "cast off."

In less than a second, David's reaching downward transforms into a descent as he falls into the arms of his kneeling, newly re-named mother. David has re-named Monica, re-activating her suspended "motherhood." But he has done so only superficially—in name only. Monica has empowered him to re-name, and ultimately re-flesh her as a mother. She has activated his embrace. David *kneels* in the *kneeling* Monica's lap and whispers, "You are my Mommy." At this moment of technological authentication, Monica completely envelopes him in a nurturing, loving embrace. The entire "descent" of David—from the point where she asks David who she is, to the point where she completely envelops him—takes less than six seconds.

In six seconds, all of David's artificiality, awkwardness, and general "creepiness" is erased by what Monica perceives as his needing her. Monica has successfully projected *her need* onto the technological other, making it seem as if *it has acknowledged her*. She does so without fully knowing or understanding the implications of her actions. She has not simply activated David's ability to love, she has also handed over her narrative to him as he becomes the perfect, loving son that he was programmed to be. David loves unconditionally, and, by the letter of his programming, *perfectly*. The difficulty arises when Monica cannot perfectly return his love. The perfect machine attempts to love the imperfect human, but the imperfect human cannot make herself *fully compatible* with David's love. The human fails the superior technological other. After several unsuccessful attempts on David's part to "make Monica love him," she abandons him in the woods, where the film then chronicles his journey to find the "blue fairy" who will transform David into a "real boy."[5]

David here represents the very human desire to see our own suffering reflected in the technological other. Although David is perfect, he still desires to be human (and thus, flawed). He sees the human as something to which he should aspire. This pattern of projection follows Scarry's model of how a "savior" figure is created in various religious traditions: humans empower the superior other to such an extent that it becomes unreachable. Thus, humans "revise" the religious narrative so that an aspect of the divine can more closely share in human suffering.

Posthuman Envy: A Memory Recovered

At the conclusion of *A.I.*, we find that David's quest has brought him both figuratively and literally to the "end of the world." After a journey that brought him face-to-face with his human creator, Dr. Hobby, David is told that the "blue fairy" is simply a fairy tale—a kind of embedded homing program designed to bring him back to his point of origin. Unable to come to terms with his own artificiality, he throws himself into the very sea which has consumed so much of civilization itself.

David, however, survives. Submerged under the sea for 2,000 years, he lives through an ice age and the extinction of humanity. His hope of becoming "fully human" keeps him alive. We must not forget that this is a very *human* hope that David possesses. But, cinematically speaking, this human hope was lifted out of the human race itself, and placed into a machine. David is encased in ice—mimicking the "pending" nature of Martin, only to be revived by what appears to be *embodied posthumans* or cyborgs. Although their exact origins are unclear, their ability to communicate and manipulate technological systems is clearly posthuman.[6] They can easily share thoughts in their entirety by simply touching each other—thereby eradicating Scarry's human "suffering" that occurs due to the unsharability of our internal states and thoughts. They are the genderless, ethereal cyborgs whom Haraway proposes. And they seem to have only one purpose: to glorify the humans who preceded them, remembering humanity and acknowledging the uniqueness of the human race. It seems that only humanity can explain "the meaning" of existence. The "specialist" explains:

> "I often felt a sort of envy of human beings and that thing they call 'spirit.'
> Human beings had created a million explanations of the meaning of life in art,
> in poetry, in mathematical formulas. Certainly, human beings must be the key
> to the meaning of existence, but human beings no longer existed."

The posthumans seem lost without their human ancestors, so much so that they began a "project" to recreate humans individually from the DNA fragments found in mummified human corpses. The only problem was that re-animated humans could only survive for one day, and then never be revived.[7] Like Jack Gladney's notion that the dead "dream" the living, the memory traces of humanity remained imprinted not only in human genetic material, but imprinted in the very "fabric" of the universe, which, according to the "specialist," stores every event that has occurred in the past.

Human experience is privileged to such a degree, that its uniqueness (as data) becomes part of the universe itself. Through posthuman witnesses, humans have been able to make an indelible mark in the universe, despite their self-extinction. And—through their ability to express themselves without hindrance, as well as their utter devotion to humanity itself—they become the *perfect witnesses* which posthumanism so desires. What is most disturbing here is that hope itself has been "expressed" into the technological. Humanity no longer has the capacity to be responsible for its narrative.

As far as a conclusion, David is given what he has always desired. Monica is re-animated from a scrap of hair, and she lives for one day, and for one purpose: to love David unconditionally. At the end of the day, a confused but grateful Monica utters the words David needed to hear:

> MONICA. I really ought to be tucking you in. Strange. Hmm. . . . How fascinating. I can hardly keep my eyes open. I don't know what's come over me. Such a beautiful day. I love you David. I do love you. I have always loved you.

At this point, the narrator explains that this moment was "the everlasting moment [David] had been waiting for." David then falls asleep next to Monica, and, for the first time, goes "to that place where dreams are born."

David, a technological being, seeks only the fulfillment of his program. The "happy ending" at which he arrives is ultimately in service of humanity itself. He was able to carry a human narrative, and bridge a gap between humanity and its assumed posthuman progeny.

Notes

All quotations in the Conclusion from *A.I. Artificial Intelligence*, DVD, directed by Steven Spielberg (2002; Universal City, CA: Dreamworks Home Entertainment, 2003).

1. Even though Martin eventually does return home, his fragility is highlighted by the presence of David's own perfection. Martin seems to be the only character who understands David's nature as "mecha" and his own replacement. Martin eventually plants doubt in his parents' minds regarding David's perfection. His plot to have David ejected from the family is successful, but only superficially. Once David is expelled, the audience never sees Martin again.

2. David's definition of love is simplistic, but is based primarily on his own status of being "unique." He explains to his temporary mecha protector, "Gigolo Joe," that he is loved: "Because I'm special, and . . . unique! Because there has never been anyone like me before! Ever! Mommy loves Martin because he is real and when I am real, Mommy's going to read to me, and tuck me in my bed, and sing to me, and listen to what I say, and she will cuddle with me, and tell me every day a hundred times a day that she loves me!"

3. Especially when he opens up the bathroom door to find Monica sitting on the toilet.

4. In a truly moving performance, Haley Joel Osment manages to very slightly—and very slowly—change his expression: at the start of the procedure he is sitting up straight, wearing a very subtle smile, but blankly looking forward. During the procedure, however,

the smile fades and his lips part slightly, and he almost imperceptibly slouches, creating a sense of vulnerability and intimacy.

5. Desperate to garner Monica's love, David listens to the advice of Martin, who tells him that she will love him if he cuts off a lock of her hair while she's asleep. Of course, Monica wakes up to see a scissor-wielding David standing over her. In her panic, she turns into the scissors and scratches her eye. Prior to that, David douses himself in his mother's now-discontinued Chanel No. 5 in order to smell "lovely," mimicking his father's declaration of love to Monica before a party.

6. The fact that their origins are never explained only further supports the active forgetting that occurs when humans empower machines: these posthumans just exist, and there is no explanation given as to how or when they came into being (or how they were activated).

7. It is interesting that only *after* the human race is extinct does the importance and uniqueness of human biology come to bear. It is also part of a very posthuman mythology that a human being—trace memories and all—can be recreated from a single recovered strand of DNA. This further supports Hayles's observation that the most basic posthuman assumption is the primacy of information and code.

Epilogue

Concluding Humanity

Posthumanism's initial gesture toward the machine—its initial movement toward a technological other—is an act of faith and submission. By surrendering responsibility, posthumanism creates a superior other who can acknowledge, protect, and complete its human creator. Hayles tells us that we stand at a point in history when we can "re-flesh" ourselves in light of ongoing technological development and celebrate our finitude as human beings. The problem is that Hayles inadvertently privileges an instrumental view of technology, and not necessarily the *biological human*. By equating all physicality as informational instantiation, it is possible that created objects can seamlessly "extend" the human. This makes possible Oedipa Maas's feelings of inadequacy and search for the "apparatus" which will allow her to execute Inverarity's will. This also makes possible the outsourcing of subjectivity from which Jack Gladney, and the technified human, suffer.

As human biology is increasingly viewed as a manifestation of code, the last bastion of humanity becomes the narrative. It remains the final "skill" that stands to be given over to the machine. As Lyotard tells us, we take in the world technologically (by sorting through and processing information), but we make sense of the world narratively. It is no surprise then, that Jack—being the most contemporary example of the posthuman—so fears the power of the narrative itself. It unites, reveals, and concludes. It is the alternative to aimless wandering. It is also the way to mark our mortality. All of our human plots come to an end. It is the "end" that posthumanism actually resists, by characterizing our constant striving and aspiring to technological models as our most human characteristic. To remain human, we must keep striving toward technological perfection.

If we remain blind to the power we invest in technology, realistically speaking, we run the risk of destroying ourselves by investing technology with more human traits and abilities, outsourcing more of our "skill" into technological systems. Taking responsibility for our technology, of course, means that we need to understand the environmental, physiological, and psychological effects of a growing dependence on machines we don't understand. Not many—not even posthumanists themselves—would disagree. But what is so vexing about posthumanism is its assumption that the technological systems which *we create* are always already superior. It is blind to the fact that technology is itself an

131

expression of human suffering, and a way to make ourselves "more available" to each other and to the world.

Although Hayles outlines the basic assumptions of posthumanism, there is one underlying assumption that remains hidden: the un-supplemented human is obsolete, and always has been. By declaring that "we are already posthuman," posthuman discourse attempts to bring the human to a close, so that it may occupy that "middle space" where it perpetually strives for an unreachable goal. Posthumanism does not call for self-destruction, but it assumes that our only hope for human survival lies in the very technology which threatens us. Its rhetoric mirrors end-times mentality: the end of the human is already here; the signs are around us. Repent, submit, and rejoice.

But the invoking of an end is itself an attempt to gain control. To throw up our hands and "give up" is exactly that—a giving up of responsibility. It is a means to grant technology, fate, God, or whatever superior other we can imagine, a dominion over us, freeing us of our own responsibility for our actions. Instead of calling for us to take responsibility for our empowerment of technology, posthumanism calls for us to take responsibility of the *boundaries* between ourselves and technology, reiterating the very Cartesian dualism which it vows to avoid and "work through." The "good posthuman" relies on technology as a separate other to maintain a distance that keeps the human special. The human is empowered via metaphors of grasping and embracing. Posthumanism forgets that the boundaries it speaks of were created by the human empowerment of technology. What posthumanism should be calling for is a recognition and reclaiming of responsibility for the way we empower technology itself.

Presently, the posthuman manifests itself as a subtle paradigm shift in human self-image. Although realistically speaking, we may not look to technology as a god-like entity, we slowly empower it in ways in which we are not even aware. We shift blame for our failures to our machines. We hide behind e-mail and voice mail. Even obsessive compulsive ticks are "technified": instead of washing our hands, we check our e-mail or voice mail repeatedly. Which washing will make us clean? Which message will make us complete? Ultimately, however, we run the risk of prematurely expecting and accepting our individual and collective obsolescence by allowing our technological systems to define our human subjectivity. The transcendence which posthumanism looks for is actually a way to give up responsibility for being human.

Posthumanism's own privileging of information and belief that it is fully transferable between substrates enables the fear that technology—under its own power—can reach a level of complexity that rivals or surpasses humanity's own. The possibility then arises that a sentient machine, with its own goals and technological ontology might eclipse humanity. If the last bastion of humanity is making meaning through narrative, we are already poised to outsource that skill to onto machines.

Posthumanism has the potential to be a discourse that can more fully address the power structure inherent in humanity's relationship to technology, but only if it acknowledges the ontological and epistemological connection between humanity and technology that has always been present. Failure to do so renders us blind to the reasons why we empower technology in the first place, and makes us vulnerable to our own fear that technology is already superior to us. If we are already posthuman, it is because we have allowed ourselves to become so. It is not simply a question of taking responsibility for the boundary between ourselves and technology; we must take responsibility for its creation.

Selected Bibliography

A.I. Artificial Intelligence, DVD. Directed by Steven Spielberg, 2002, Universal City, CA: Dreamworks Home Entertainment, 2003.

Badmington, Neil. "Theorizing Posthumanism." *Cultural Critique* 53 (2003): 10-27.

Breger, Louis. *Freud: Darkness in the Midst of Vision*. New York: John Wiley & Sons, Inc., 2000.

DeLillo, Don. *White Noise*. New York: Penguin Books, 1986.

Descartes, Rene. *Discourse on the Method of Rightly Conducting One's Reason and Seeing the Truth in the Sciences*. In *Descartes: Selected Philosophical Writings*. Edited and translated by John Cottingham, Robert Stoothoff, and Dugald Murdoch, 20-56. Cambridge and New York: Cambridge University Press, 1988.

———. *Meditations on First Philosophy in Which Are Demonstrated The Existence of God and the Distinction between the Human Soul and the Body*. In *Descartes: Selected Philosophical Writings*. Edited and translated by John Cottingham, Robert Stoothoff, and Dugald Murdoch, 73-122. Cambridge and New York: Cambridge University Press, 1988.

Eddins, Dwight. *The Gnostic Pynchon*. Bloomington: Indiana University Press, 1990.

Elder, Charles R. *The Grammar of the Unconscious*. University Park: The Pennsylvania State University Press, 1994.

Freud, Sigmund. "Analysis Terminable and Interminable." In *The Standard Edition of the Complete Psychological Works of Sigmund Freud*. Edited and Translated by James Strachey et al., vol. 23. London: Hogarth Press, 1953-74.

———. "Beyond the Pleasure Principle." In *The Standard Edition of the Complete Psychological Works of Sigmund Freud*. Edited and translated by James Strachey et al., vol. 18. London: Hogarth Press, 1953-74.

———. "Introductory Lectures on Psychoanalysis." In *The Standard Edition of the Complete Psychological Works of Sigmund Freud*. Edited and translated by James Strachey et al., vols. 15-16. London: Hogarth Press, 1953-74.

Hansen, Mark. *Embodying Technisis: Technology Beyond Writing*. Ann Arbor, MI: The University of Michigan Press, 2000.

Haraway, Donna J. *Simians, Cyborgs, and Women: The Reinvention of Nature*. New York: Routledge, 1991.

———. *ModestWiness@Second_Millenium.FemaleMan©_Meets_OncoMouse: Feminism and Technoscience*. New York: Routledge, 1997.

Harris, Paul. "Thinking @ The Speed of Time: Globalization and Its Dis-Contents or, Can Lyotard's Thought Go on Without a Body?" *Yale French Studies* 99 (2001): 129-148.

Hayles, N. Katherine. *How We Became Posthuman: Virtual Bodies in Cybernetics, Literature, and Informatics*. Chicago: The University of Chicago Press, 1999.

———. *My Mother Was a Computer: Digital Subjects and Literary Texts*. Chicago: The University of Chicago Press, 2005.

Heidegger, Martin. "The Question Concerning Technology." *The Question Concerning Technology and Other Essays*. Trans. William Lovitt. New York: Harper & Row, 1977.

Leps, Marie Christine. "Empowerment Through Information: A Discursive Critique." *Cultural Critique* 31 (1995): 179-96.

Lyotard, Jean-François. *The Inhuman: Reflections on Time*. Trans. Geoffrey Bennington and Rachel Bowlby. Stanford: Stanford University Press, 1991.

Nicholls, Peter. "Divergences: Modernism, Postmodernism, Jameson and Lyotard." *Critical Quarterly* 33.3 (1991): 1-18.

O'Donnell, Patrick. "Engendering Paranoia in Contemporary Narrative." *Boundary 2* 19.1 (1992): 181-204.

Pynchon, Thomas. *The Crying of Lot 49*. New York: Harper and Row, 1966.

Scarry, Elaine. *The Body in Pain: The Making and Unmaking of the World*. New York: Oxford University Press, 1985.

Schaub, Thomas Hill. *Pynchon: The Voice of Ambiguity*. Urbana: University of Illinois Press, 1981.

Seed, David. *The Fictional Labyrinths of Thomas Pynchon*. London: MacMillan Press, 1988.

Thacker, Eugene. "Data Made Flesh: Biotechnology and the Discourse of the Posthuman." *Cultural Critique* 53 (2003): 72-97.

Wilcox, Leonard. "Boudrillard, DeLillo's *White Noise*, and the End of Heroic Narrative." *Contemporary Literature* 32.3 (1991): 345-65.

Wilde, Alan. *Middle Grounds: Studies in Contemporary American Fiction*. Philadelphia: University of Pennsylvania Press, 1987.

Zuern, John. "Martin Heidegger: The Question Concerning Technology." *Criticalink*. 1998. University of Hawaii at Manoa. 8 Aug. 2005 http://www2.hawaii.edu/~zuern/demo/heidegger/.

Index

*Embodying Technesis: Technology
  Beyond Writing*, 31n21
enclosing, 5
encoding, 46
enframing, 62, 67-68, 69-70, 86, 105
entropy, 74
epistemology, 1, 23, 62, 81
evolution, 61
expression, 78-79, 105
extropian posthumanism, 7, 11

faith, 79-81, 105, 112, 131
finitude, 4, 5, 61
Freud, Sigmund, 7, 53, 74, 77, 79-80,
  83-94, 97, 105. *See also* "Analysis
  Terminable and Interminable"

Gladney, Jack, 12, 55, 107-120, 125,
  126, 127, 128, 131; and search for
  apparatus, 107, 110, 117; and in-
  adequacy/inferiority, 108, 120

Hansen, Mark B. N., ix-x, 31n21. *See
  also Embodying Technesis: Technology Beyond Writing*
Haraway, Donna, ix-xi, 12, 17, 20-24,
  25 26-28, 53, 56, 57, 60, 74, 77, 81,
  87, 90, 95, 105, 107, 109, 112, 114,
  119, 126, 128. See also "A Cyborg
  Manifesto: Science, Technology,
  and Socialist-Feminism in the Late
  Twentieth Century"
Harris, Paul, 79, 80
Hayles, N. Katherine, ix-xi, 1, 3-12, 17,
  21, 22, 23, 27, 53, 55, 56, 57, 60,
  61, 67, 69, 74, 81, 83, 87, 90, 96,
  105-106, 108, 126, 131-32. See Also, *How We Became Posthuman:
  Virtual Bodies in Cybernetics, Literature, and Informatics*
Heidegger, Martin, xi, 12, 62-72, 74,
  76, 80-81, 91-92, 95, 96, 106, 110-
  11, 115, 119. *See also The Question
  Concerning Technology*
Herausfordern, 65, 110
*How We Became Posthuman: Virtual
  Bodies in Cybernetics, Literature,
  and Informatics*, 2, 3, 17, 22, 54
humanism, 36, 4, 53, 54-55, 59, 60-61,
  69, 72, 73, 81, 91

hubris, 29, 112

immortality, 7, 19
interface, 3, 40, 62
information, 1, 3, 4, 9, 19-21, 29, 33,
  40, 43, 49, 55, 57-58, 60-61, 64, 66,
  69-70, 71-73, 77-80, 82, 85-88, 93,
  96-97, 105-106, 109-10, 112-17,
  123; compatibility with, 55, 72; as
  experience, 86, 96; interpretation of,
  80, 117; and manipulation, 72, 77;
  responsibility to, 114-115, 117; as
  standing-reserve, 67, 68
informed posthuman, 6, 109
The Inhuman: Reflections on Time, 24,
  70-83, 109
instantiated Information, 6, 131
interface, 9, 20, 33, 43, 48, 56, 57, 95,
  110, 126
Inverarity, Pierce, 34, 48

liberal humanist subject, ix, 3, 4, 5, 11,
  18, 19, 20, 22, 56, 71, 73, 78, 82,
  90, 119
logos, x, 31n21
Lyotard, Jean-Francois, x, xi, 12, 24,
  53, 70-81, 82, 86, 91-92, 94, 97,
  105, 106, 109, 110, 115, 117, 119,
  124, 131. *See also The Inhuman:
  Reflections on Time*

Maas, Oedipa, 12, 23, 33-49; and appa-
  ratus, 35, 44; and feelings of inade-
  quacy, 37, 45-49
Macy Conferences, 13n5
materiality, 4
Maxwell's Demon, 43-44
McCulloch, Warren, 13n5
*Modest_Witness@Second_Millenium.
  FemaleMan©_Meets_Onco
  Mouse™:Feminism and Technos-
  cience*, x
My Mother Was a Computer, ix

narrative, 48, 54, 70-77, 78-80, 81, 83-
  85, 88, 95-96, 105-106, 117, 119,
  124, 126-27, 131
Nefastis Machine, 43, 44, 45, 119, 125,
  126
Nyodene-D, 113

About the Author

Anthony Miccoli is currently the Director of Philosophy and an assistant professor of communication and philosophy at Western State College of Colorado. His main interests are posthumanism, the philosophy of technology, epistemology, phenomenology, as well as literary theory and cultural studies. He has taught courses in philosophy, communication, and English.

Breinigsville, PA USA
10 January 2010
230465BV00004B/1/P